Praise for Russ Johnson, Ph.D., and Usa Johnson's *Absolutely* Everything *You Need to Know About Prospecting*

This book will become the gold standard of network prospecting. The Johnsons have left no stone unturned in their marvelous effort to arm both the novice and seasoned veteran with a tremendous road map to unlimited wealth.

> — Mark Yarnell, industry leader and author of *Your Best Year in Network Marketing*

Russ and Usa Johnson have provided the most complete resource on prospecting ever. It even goes beyond teaching "absolutely everything you need to know" about this important skill.

> — Keith Laggos, Ph.D., publisher of *Money Maker's Monthly* and *The Direct Sales Journal*, and author of *Direct Sales: An Overview*

As top bananas in network marketing, Russ and Usa speak from experience. They offer good tips you can use today.

> — Kim Klaver, president of Max Out Productions and author of *Do You Have a Plan B? A guide to an alternative career in direct sales and network marketing*

The 21-Day Challenge

Launch your network marketing empire in three weeks!

Russ Johnson, Ph.D., and Usa Johnson

with Beth Mende Conny, M.A.

The 21-Day Challenge: Launch your network marketing empire in three weeks!

To order additional copies of this book online, visit:
TheProspectPro.com

To place bulk orders of *The 21-Day Challenge*, contact:
Beth Mende Conny
Biz Builders Consulting, LLC
P.O. Box 1936
Frederick, MD 21702
301/694-9921
orders@BizBuildersConsulting.com

To contact the authors:
Russ Johnson, Ph.D., and Usa Johnson
P.O. Box 880305
Boca Raton, FL 33488-305
561/391-1647

Cover design by JeanPetersonDesign.com

Contents

Ready, set, go!

In 2003, we released the critically acclaimed book *Absolutely Everything You Need to Know About Prospecting: The winning strategies today's top earners use to make friends, recruit distributors and build their network marketing empires.* The phenomenal response to the book heartened us and reaffirmed our commitment to helping network marketers worldwide achieve lifelong prosperity. The book you now hold was born of that commitment.

The 21-Day Challenge: Launch your network marketing empire in three weeks! has one goal: to turn you into a network marketing powerhouse. Its 21 Challenges are filled with invaluable strategies for achieving unparalleled success — the very strategies today's top earners use to build their empires. How we wish we had had this book when we first launched our businesses!

Read a chapter a day for the next three weeks, and you will have EVERYTHING you need to know about launching and expanding your business!

If you're new to network marketing, take note: The information we present will flatten your learning curve and build your confidence. Better yet, it will create a blueprint that will help you chart your course and set ambitious, but realistic, goals.

If you're a veteran network marketer, take note: This book will allow you to rediscover winning strategies while learning new techniques. The book also is a great tool for training your downline and increasing retention. As a result, you'll be able to grow your business that much more quickly.

The 21-Day Challenge, one week at a time

Before you jump into the book, we'd like to tell you how it's organized so you can get the most out of it.

The 21 Challenges are grouped by week, seven per week. **Week 1 Challenges** lay the foundation for your network marketing success. Here, you'll take one key step at a time, gaining a deeper understanding of the industry, your company and products — and yourself! You'll also learn more about us. As our stories attest, we started with nothing. It is our hope that they will inspire you.

Week 2 Challenges are designed to get you into action. They'll take you through the steps of identifying prospects, creating a winning presentation and working with your upline to get the support you need.

Week 3 Challenges will take you to a higher level in your professional development. You'll be presented with the more advanced strategies industry leaders use to expand their empires. (Even veteran marketers can learn a trick or two here!) You'll also be given tips for creating the positive mind-set so critical to your success.

Four ways to get the most from this book

First, skim the book, to get an overview of the material covered and see how each Challenge builds on the previous one. You should then proceed sequentially.

Second, clear your calendar. We want you to schedule time each day to read a Challenge, one a day for the next three weeks. Don't allow yourself excuses: "I'm too busy today" or "I'll have to start next week or month." If this is too much of a commitment, don't bother reading another word of this book. Network marketing isn't for you. It only works for people who commit to their own success.

Third, read each Challenge more than once — ideally, three to five times, as studies show that repetition greatly increases retention. Ideally, space your readings out over the course of a day, such as first thing in the morning, during lunch and just before you go to bed.

Fourth, take action! At the end of each chapter, we suggest specific actions that will energize and provide you with a personalized game plan for success. Also pay attention to our suggested readings. They refer you to related sections in our book *Absolutely Everything You Need to Know About Prospecting,* as well as to other great books that will deepen your knowledge and strengthen your skills. You'll also find a bibliography of great titles on Pages 103–106.

Enough said. Let the Challenge begin!

Take note! (or should we say notes?)

Throughout the 21-Day Challenge, you'll be asked to jot down your ideas, strategies and goals. We suggest that you purchase a notebook for just this purpose. It's a handy way to put all your thoughts under one roof, so to speak. It also allows you an easy way to review individual components of your personalized action plan. *Buy your notebook today!*

Words of wisdom

Your right to life means your right to have the free and unrestricted use of all the things which may be necessary to your fullest mental, spiritual and physical unfoldment. In other words, you have a right to be rich.
— Wallace D. Wattles, *The Science of Getting Rich*

For those of you who are considering embarking on your own financial fast track, you may have some doubts about your abilities. All I can say is trust that you have everything you need right now to be successful financially. All it takes to bring out your natural God-given gifts is your desire, determination and a deep faith that you have a genius and a gift that is unique.
— Robert T. Kiyosaki, *The CASHFLOW Quadrant*

You may as well know, right here, that you can never have riches in great quantities unless you can work yourself into a white heat of desire for money, and actually believe you will possess it.
— Napoleon Hill, *Think and Grow Rich*

Let a man radically alter his thoughts, and he will be astonished at the rapid transformation it will effect in the material conditions of his life. Men imagine that thought can be kept secret, but it cannot; it rapidly crystallizes into habit, and habit solidifies into circumstance.
— James Allen, *As a Man Thinketh*

Week 1

1. Pick up your shovel (Part 1)

2. Pick up your shovel (Part 2)

3. Pinpoint your dreams

4. Commit to your success

5. Become an expert

6. Become a myth-buster

7. Fall in love with your company and products

Challenge #1
Pick up your shovel (Part 1)

We begin our first two Challenges with the stories of how each of us came to network marketing. As you will see, the road to our success was full of twists and turns and difficult times. Still, we persevered, as we hope you will. We share our stories so you will know us better and see how we are just like you. We weren't born with silver spoons in our mouths; nor did we have an inside edge. We are self-made.

We're proud of all we've achieved. More importantly, we're enjoying the fruits of our labor. We planted the seeds of our success not terribly long ago, watered them with faith and effort, and watched them grow. You too can have a plentiful garden. Simply pick up your shovel and work the soil until you hit pay dirt.

Usa's story

I was born in Bangkok, Thailand, into a modest and traditional family. Like other women of my generation, I was expected to marry and raise children. I wanted to do both, yet I wanted more. I wanted an exciting career and great wealth; I wanted to better the lives of others. And that was just for starters! Although I longed to share my dreams with others, I knew they'd ridicule me. "Such crazy ideas," I could hear them say. "And from a woman, no less."

It's not surprising then that I did what was expected. I married and had a child. Within a few years, however, my life began taking some unexpected turns.

First, after several years of marriage, my husband and I divorced. Although this is hard for any woman, it was particularly hard given the traditional nature of my culture and the fact that I was suddenly thrown into the workforce. Supporting my son was

15

my first and only priority. Any dreams I had had while younger were pushed aside. Permanently, I thought.

Luckily, I was able to secure a job as a secretary for the Thai bar association. I say luckily, because it not only provided me with the steady income I needed to raise my son, but also created great feelings of dissatisfaction. I, for one, happen to think that dissatisfaction can be a positive thing if it moves you closer to what you want. This is exactly what happened to me. Increasingly, I began to think about what I wanted out of life. Surely, there had to be more than working so many hours for so little pay. But what more was there, and how could I find it? I didn't know the answers, but I had a sense of where to look.

More and more, I began dusting off my dreams of wealth and happiness and thinking of starting my life anew, in a place I believed held great promise: the United States. If other immigrants could go there and achieve financial success, so could I. It would take time, it would take effort, but I would at least try.

First, however, I had to deal with the negative responses of others. My family couldn't believe I'd do such a crazy thing. "How will you manage?" they cried. "You've got no money, no place to stay." Even my ex-husband joined in the chorus. "Who do you think you are?" he said. "You'll never be anything more than a secretary." It was difficult to counter their arguments. I was asking the same questions myself.

Nonetheless, I packed my bags, filling them with dreams, fears and photos of my son, whom I left behind in his grandparents' care. "I will return for you as soon as I can make a better life for us," I told him tearfully. Whether it was his wishful heart or unfailing love for his mother, he took my words as a promise. Wanting to prove worthy of his trust, I set off into the great unknown. It was the spring of 1989.

Into the great unknown

America truly was a great unknown. Not only was the culture alien to me, but I spoke little English. What had I gotten myself into?

Upon arrival, I stayed in Las Vegas with a Thai friend who had previously moved to the States. Through her, I found work in California, first as a baby-sitter and then as a restaurant worker. I worked from 11 a.m. to 11 p.m., seven days a week, 52 weeks a year, with only one day off — Christmas. My take-home pay was $200 a week, not even enough to meet my living expenses. It was one of the most difficult and depressing times of my life. Had I really left Thailand for this? At times I thought of swallowing my pride and returning home. But then I'd think about my son, how patiently he was still waiting for me and the better life I had promised. No, I decided. I wouldn't return. Somehow I'd find a better way; somehow I'd get a decent job and life. I'd make my dreams come true.

A roll of the dice

In 1991, I moved back to Las Vegas, and it was there that my life took another unexpected turn — this one for the better. It was as if I had rolled some cosmic dice and come up a winner (and what better place to roll the dice than Vegas!). It all began with a phone call.

I was at my friend's house when a man with the most melodious voice called, the kind of voice you hear only on the radio. My friend was out at the time (a fact I tried to explain to the caller in my broken English), and so I took a message. The caller's name was Russell Johnson. Little did I know that I'd be signing my name Usa Johnson within the year.

As it turned out, Russ had a great radio voice because he had been on radio for years. In fact, he had his own business show on American Radio Network. Apparently, my friend had heard a segment Russ did on network marketing (whatever the heck that was!) and contacted him for more information. Upon returning home, my friend immediately called Columbia, Maryland, where Russ lived and worked. They chatted for quite some time, first about network marketing and then … about me.

Russ, it seemed, had liked the sound of my voice and the person behind the heavy accent. (I guess being in radio allowed him to pick up on things most other folks can't.) I was flattered and flabbergasted. In that one conversation with my friend, Russ learned my short and somewhat sad little story: how I had come to this country in search of a better life and how I had been working horrid jobs under horrid conditions. Russ was sympathetic. He too had been through tough times and his share of low-paying jobs. He admired my spunk and determination to achieve great wealth and happiness. As I would soon learn, he was determined to do the same.

Over the following weeks, my friend and Russ continued to talk. Inevitably, the conversation turned toward me. "How's she doing?" Russ would ask. "Has she gotten her green card yet?" My friend would answer: "She's still struggling, and no, she hasn't gotten her card." Ultimately, Russ thought of a solution to my problems — we could marry.

Russ, it just so happened, was a widower who had been hoping just the right woman would come along. Thinking I might be the one, he suggested I fly out sometime to visit him. If we hit it off, we could marry. And if we didn't … well, we could marry anyway. He wanted me to get a green card and a good shot at life.

To make a long story short, I flew east a few weeks later. We hit it off beautifully and married a few months later. I not only got a wedding band but an unexpected gift: an introduction to the exciting, incredibly profitable world of network marketing.

Prospecting 101

Russ had long been a believer in network marketing, having been in the business some 20-plus years. He had managed to support himself at it for the last 10 years, but only barely. And yet he persevered. "You've got to try this, Usa," he would say. "Let's work a business together." But I kept putting him off. Me sell anything to anyone? Ha! Marriage might have made my life easier, but it hadn't made me less shy or any braver. "What do you have to lose?" he'd persist. "Do you want to keep working the way you're working now? What kind of future is that for you or us?"

Russ had a point, and an obvious one at that. He was just starting out with a new network marketing company at the time, and while he was fully committed to making it go, there was still the initial lean stretch ahead. To make ends meet, I worked days at McDonald's and nights at Taco Bell, making $5 an hour. At the rate I was going, my son would be a senior citizen before I could bring him to the States! I had nothing to lose. I'd give network marketing a try.

Now, if this were a Hollywood movie, I would have become an overnight success. Unfortunately, I was still just me — a former fast-food worker who spoke broken English and was scared silly. And those were my good qualities! Each day it seemed I added yet another item to my shortcomings list. Talk about a negative mind-set!

One of my problems was that I mistakenly believed you had to be a life-of-the-party type who could walk up to a stranger and sign him or her on the spot. That it took me three, four or even 10-plus times to recruit a distributor was dispiriting; that I got so many more nos than yeses was downright devastating.

Russ tried to talk some sense into me. "Success is like a muscle," he'd say. "You've got to build it over time. Besides, getting a whole lot of yeses doesn't mean you've built a strong organization. People who say yes too quickly often give up too quickly, especially those new to the industry.

"And another thing: You don't have to be an extrovert, intro-vert or an in-betweenvert to make it in this business. Just be your-self. You've got so many prospecting tools at your disposal. Find the ones you're most comfortable with, then grow into others. And don't forget to develop your own. You are your greatest asset, Lisa. Take stock of your strengths and build on them."

Buoyed by Russ' words, I began to experiment with various prospecting strategies, trying to find the ones that fit best. I quick-ly realized that some worked better than others in certain settings or among certain types of people. As obvious as that might sound, it was a revelation: I had been trying to find a one-size-fits-all tech-nique when there was none. That lesson learned, I began to build my success muscle.

A timely introduction

In 1994, Russ joined a new network marketing company and I began working it with him.* Two years later, we were drawing a six-figure income. My days of flipping burgers and stuffing taco shells were over at last.

That's not the end of my story, however. A couple of years later, my life took another unexpected turn. Again, it came by way of a phone call.

The call was from an acquaintance of Russ', an extraordinarily successful businessman named Tom, whom my husband greatly admired. Although Tom had already made his fortune, he had long been sold on the network marketing model and had worked for

---

* *Technically, Russ had joined the business in 1986, but it had taken about eight years for the state of Maryland to formally recognize the company. Talk about bureaucracies — and how damaging misconceptions about the network mar-keting industry can be!*

several companies, building downlines in the tens of thousands and drawing annual salaries in the six-figures. Tom had just become one of the very first distributors for a new and promising company that offered a unique line of health products. "I'd like you to join my organization," he told Russ. "It's a winner."

Russ believed him, knowing that Tom wouldn't put his prodigious energy into anything that didn't have great potential. We weren't particularly interested in joining another company, however. We were already committed to our present company and were, at last, seeing the fruits of our labor. We decided to sample the products, nonetheless, if only to see what the fuss was about. If we liked them, we might consider wholesaling them. After a few weeks of sampling, I noticed that some of my little aches and pains were gone. Still, I wasn't convinced and dismissed it as coincidence.

On my own

Right about this time, I was scheduled to visit my son in Thailand. Almost as an afterthought, I brought along the remainder of my samples for friends to try. It was only after their enthusiastic thumbs-up that I began to turn a more serious eye on the products. After returning to the States, my wholesale business started booming and my commission checks kept growing. "Hmmm," I thought. "I'm going to take a closer look at this company!" I liked what I saw.

Soon after, I decided to launch my own business with this company. Several factors came into play. First, the opportunity seemed like a great one: The company and products were solid, and it would be lucrative and exciting to be among the very first of its distributors. Second, I wanted to test my wings. I had gained so much confidence working with Russ, yet I still wondered if I could make it on my own. There was only one way to find out.

Third, the timing of my launch was right for Russ as well.

Although he was still expanding the organization we had built together, he began to devote an increasing amount of time to helping network marketers worldwide achieve success through both tried-and-true and cutting-edge prospecting techniques. Of equal importance, he wanted to spread the word about the promise and legitimacy of network marketing. He had long grown tired of how the industry had been disparaged. He believed it to be a way for people around the world to achieve prosperity, and it was his mission to spread the word.

With these considerations in mind, I set out my own shingle, using the prospecting techniques that had served me so well in the past, the very techniques mentioned in *Absolutely* Everything *You Need to Know About Prospecting*. I built my business steadily, and before I knew it, had a downline in the thousands and was earning a six-figure income. My American dream had come true.

Today's challenge

In your notebook, write down the story of *your* life. It doesn't have to be well-written or even in complete sentences. The goal is to trace the events that led you to where you are now. What challenges did you face? What lessons did you learn? What strengths did you develop? How can you use each of them to launch your network marketing career?

Suggested readings: Now that you've read the story of my life and written about yours, it's time to read about the lives of others. Go beyond network marketers, however. The world is full of inspiring individuals who achieved success only after they looked fear and doubt in the face. Just recently, for example, I read the autobiography of the renowned violinist Isaac Stern.* As difficult as it may be to believe, one of his very first concert reviews pro-

---

* *Stern, Isaac, with Chaim Potok* — Isaac Stern: My first 79 years.

22

nounced him mediocre and even questioned his skills. Devastated, Stern climbed aboard a city bus and rode for six hours, trying to decide whether to stay the course or pack it in. Ultimately, he held firm. Thank goodness. The world would be an emptier place without people like him — and you!

Challenge #2
Pick up your shovel! (Part 2)

Russ' story

I was born in Baltimore, Maryland, and as anyone who knows me will tell you, I've always been one to jump into new experiences and make the best of them. For this I have to thank my parents. My father was a pastor, my mother a homemaker, and they stressed the importance of faith and a positive attitude. I could do anything I wanted in life, they told me, and I believed them.

My parents separated when I was 10. My mother had a hard time making ends meet, so I moved around a bit, living with my aunts, cousins and grandparents, and for a time, in a boys home. I also spent a couple of years with a pastor and his wife who lived on a farm in Virginia. I'd get up at 5 a.m., milk the cows, feed the chickens, chop wood, get a fire going and do whatever else needed to be done. I was a teen then and it wasn't exactly my idea of fun — the farm didn't even have indoor plumbing — but I came out ahead. The experience reaffirmed my faith, helped me develop a strong work ethic and got me in the habit of waking early. (Even today I'm up by dawn to get the most out of each day.)

Off to war

After my stint on the farm, I returned to Baltimore. My mother had remarried by then. My stepfather and I didn't get along particularly well. What was more difficult, however, was that I was held back a grade when I re-entered the city's school system. The Korean War was going on at the time, so I dropped out and enlisted in the Air Force. (The clerk who processed my paperwork apparently didn't care that I was just 16.)

Going into the service, I was given an IQ test, and I and scored better than impressively. My supervisors were surprised as much as I was. I mean, here's this kid who never graduated from high school. Because I had scored particularly well in electronics, I was trained as a control tower operator. The assignment required razor-sharp focus, but I thrived on the challenge. By the time I was 18, I had become a supervisor.

I was stationed in the States for a while and then shipped off to Japan, where I lived for two years. It was my first exposure to Asian culture — any foreign culture, for that matter — and I was impressed by the quiet dignity of the people and how hard they worked.

The service also was my first exposure to so many educated people. One fellow I knew was a graduate of New York University, a real sharp guy. Back in the barracks, he'd rib me for spending so much of my free time reading pulp fiction. "Why are you wasting your time?" he'd ask. "The world's full of great, important books that will shape your mind." I paid attention to him and began reading up on psychology, sociology, politics, religion — serious topics that gave me a new perspective. I now understood why my father had always pushed me to get a college education. There was a whole world out there, and a degree would open the doors to it.

There was one door I had to open first, however. I had to get my high school diploma. Luckily, the military had a GED program. I studied at night and had my diploma in hand by the time I was discharged.

A man of many hats

After leaving the service I was ready to go to college, and thanks to the GI Bill, I could.* It took awhile to finish up my

---

* First, however, I had to earn another GED, this time from the state of Maryland, which required its own diploma before admitting me to college.

coursework, however. Fifteen years, to be precise. I had left school after my second year. I was married by then and a new dad, and I needed money coming in, not going out.

During the next decade or so, I took a course here and there and worked lots of different jobs: cab driver, truck driver, bus driver, assembly-line worker, parking attendant, encyclopedia salesman, insurance salesman, janitor ... you name it. When I tell people now about what I was doing then, many shake their heads and say, "Man, you must have hated every minute." But you know, I didn't. As I said, I had a strong work ethic and whatever I was doing, I was going to do well. I also liked meeting people from all walks of life. The way I saw it, people were people. They had the same interests and needs: They all wanted to better their lives. This exposure helped me later when I began prospecting. I felt comfortable talking to just about anyone. It was as if I already knew them.

As you know, the '60s and '70s were a time of great upheaval in our country. You had love-ins, sit-ins, the black power and women's liberation movements, marches against the war and marches for civil rights. I was right in the middle of it, believing, like so many folks back then, that you could effect change through social programs for the underprivileged. Toward that end, I taught in Baltimore's inner city schools. I also was a field supervisor for the Neighborhood Youth Corps and a community organizer for the Urban League. Over time, however, I began to understand that public funds alone couldn't change the way people perceived themselves. If they labeled themselves as disadvantaged, they were going to be disadvantaged; no government program could change that. If they saw themselves as recipients, they wouldn't act on their own behalf. What they needed was a different model, one that would help them achieve self-sufficiency. I would find that model in network marketing.

A network who?

A number of years later, I was having a beer with a good buddy at a neighborhood watering hole, when he mentioned a mutual friend who was now in business for herself and doing quite well. "What's the business?" I asked. Like so many people outside of network marketing, he didn't quite understand what it was, let alone how it worked. Neither did I, but that didn't stop me from heading over to her place as soon as he and I parted. If someone was successful in business, I wanted to hear about it. I wasn't exactly rolling in the bucks, after all.

As it turned out, I arrived at her door in the middle of a home meeting. Because she was busy, she politely saw me to the door, promising to call me later. I wasn't so easily dismissed, however. I asked her to give me some materials, tapes, whatever she had that I could review in the meantime. I devoured these as soon as I got home and was at her door the next day, asking for more and to sign on as a distributor.

This company had its monthly requirements, and I'm not just talking volume here. I was expected to listen to tapes of its top earners and to read its inspirational book-of-the-month picks. Hey, no resistance from me. I had always been an avid reader, only this time, instead of pulp fiction or heavy-duty texts on heavy-duty subjects, I tore through books on how to develop a positive mental attitude.

Overnight, I became a student of success. I read biographies of John D. Rockefeller, Henry Ford, Andrew Carnegie, Henry Kaiser and hundreds of other business leaders who had built financial empires and changed the world. I read every book I could find by the masters of positive thinking: James Allen, Dale Carnegie, Earl Nightingale, Dr. Norman Vincent Peale and Maxwell Maltz, among others. I listened to self-help tapes as I exercised, drove around town and sat in doctors' offices. I soaked it all up, and yet I wasn't achieving the success I had envisioned.

I didn't get it. Network marketing seemed simple enough — you sold products to people, recruited them to do the same, and before you knew it the bucks rolled in, right?

At first, I told myself it was because I was only working the business part time, but even I didn't buy that after a while. I knew many successful network marketers who had started that way, after all. I also knew some who had launched their businesses while holding down full-time jobs. OK, if that wasn't the problem, what was?

Looking back now, I can see exactly what I was doing wrong. First, I kept jumping from one company to the next, chasing any get-rich scheme I could find. Second, I wasn't choosing the right companies. Some were take-the-money-and-run operations; others looked great on paper but quickly folded; still others had compensation plans that didn't pan out. Third, I was selling products I wasn't excited about. They weren't unique, of high enough quality or priced competitively. Fourth, I often worked more than one company at a time, dissipating my efforts. How could I sing the praises of any one of them if I wasn't working it exclusively? Fifth — and perhaps most importantly — I was thinking small. As a result, I wasn't getting the results I wanted; things were moving too slowly. Fortunately, around that time, I met Usa. At last, my personal and professional lives were on track.

Themes

If I were writing a traditional autobiography, I'd arrange everything in chronological order. But sometimes chronology doesn't give you the big picture, an accurate sense of who a person is. That's why I'd rather speak in terms of "themes," the constant strands that have shaped my life.

For example, I have always been a spiritual person. My father, like his father, was a pastor. During my impressionable teen years working on a farm, I lived with a pastor. In my 40s, I became a pastor myself. I wanted to serve God and others, to help them reach for the heavens and the best in themselves. Today, I may be more ecumenical in my approach, but my belief has never changed: We have greatness within, and it is our right — our duty — to bring it forth. That's certainly been my goal.

Another theme

As I mentioned, it took me a while to get my B.A. Nonetheless, I wanted to continue my education, so I went on to earn my master's and Ph.D. All three degrees were in communications, reflecting how much I enjoyed working in radio and TV.

I got my first media job in the early '60s as a part-time disc jockey. I had always thought it would be great to be a D.J., but I hadn't a clue as to how to go about it. Then, one night, I was at a party and met a woman who worked at an AM/FM radio station. She suggested I visit there and gave me the name of one of the D.J.s. Talk about generous people — this guy not only gave me his time, he also let me sit in the studio with him and learn the ropes. I did so for two solid weeks, at the end of which he told the station manager to hire me. The manager just happened to be launching a daily jazz show and needed a host. I jumped at the chance, even though it meant working as an assembly-line worker by day and a D.J. by night. (More precisely, I was on air from midnight to 6 a.m., six days a week.) I had a great time, and played some of the best jazz Baltimore had ever heard. Not that anyone was listening, except perhaps my mother (I hope!) and an older woman, a jazz enthusiast who was always calling in requests. Another reason my audience was small was because FM was brand new at the time. Everyone else — and I mean *everyone* else — was listening to AM. FM was considered a doomed experiment. Why, back then you could buy an FM station for a song (something I sure wish I had done)!

Pick up your shovel (Part 2)

From my first gig on, I've had a hand in the media, working full- and part-time in radio and TV, sometimes while holding down other jobs. In addition to being a D.J., I was a talk-show host, a director of special programming for National Public Radio and a TV news anchor and investigative reporter for WBAL-TV 11 in Baltimore. I taught communications at Howard, Antioch and Morgan State universities. I also served as acting general manager for WPFW-Radio, and produced and hosted a nationally syndicated business talk show for American Radio Network.

As much as I liked working in the media, I grew tired and uncomfortable with its primary focus — reporting the news, so much of which was bad. After a while, the negativity got to me. It wasn't that I wanted to bury my hand in the sand; I just didn't want to feel buried by all that could and sometimes did go wrong in the world. That wasn't the kind of world I wanted to live in, and thanks to all the success books I was reading, I knew I didn't have to. The more I read, the more my outlook changed. Instead of seeing the impossible, I saw the possible. And thanks to network marketing, I was meeting a whole lot of people who felt the same. All of us were making a conscious effort to improve our lives and help others do the same. And it was working.

Given my strong belief in the network marketing model, I found as many opportunities as I could to promote the industry. That's how I came to do a segment on it for my syndicated business show — one that caught the ear of a listener in Las Vegas, who just happened to be a friend of Usa's. (I guess not all news is bad, eh?)

Enter Usa

Usa's already told you about how we met by phone. Hearing her voice, hearing her story — my heart went out to her. I truly wanted to help her. I was also ready to remarry. My wife had passed away seven years earlier. We had been married 27 wonderful years,

31

and I no longer wanted to live alone. When I proposed to Usa, I knew it was a gamble, but I hoped for the best. If we hit it off, great. If we didn't, well, we could marry anyway, even if it meant going our separate ways. I knew how much getting a green card meant to her. Happily, we clicked, and in 1992 we tied the knot.

Usa had the quiet dignity and work ethic that had so impressed me while I was stationed in the Far East. Like me, she was determined to achieve great wealth, health and happiness. Unlike me, she wanted nothing to do with network marketing. See, Usa was incredibly shy and absolutely convinced she couldn't sell anything to anyone. I tried to explain that she didn't have to sell as much as share an opportunity, but she wouldn't budge. Eventually, though, she began to entertain the idea.

In 1994, I launched my career with a well-established network marketing company that had just opened its doors in my home state of Maryland, after eight years of bureaucratic tangles. Fortuitously, I became one of the state's very first distributors. I knew I had struck gold. It offered a product line that had no competition. Its training program and compensation plan were great. Better still, I was recruited by an industry veteran. His track record was impressive. That he gave the company his stamp of approval meant it was a sure thing. And so for the first time in my career, I was ready to give 100 percent-plus to building an incredibly wide and deep organization. Ultimately, I became one of the company's top earners, generating 40 percent of my sponsor's earnings.

That was down the road, however. In the meantime, Usa and I had to make ends meet. She worked at McDonald's by day and Taco Bell by night. This got pretty old, pretty fast, and by force, rather than enthusiasm, she agreed to give network marketing a try. From that point on, our business grew exponentially.

Working together, Usa and I were an unstoppable team. Our synergy built our business beyond our wildest expectations. We gave it our absolute all, putting in long hours, setting ambitious goals and putting in even longer hours. Within a year, we were making a six-figure income. Shy, quiet Usa had become a power-house. She could now talk to anyone, anywhere, and in 1996 was ready to go out on her own.

As she mentioned earlier, we got a call that year from an acquaintance of mine, Tom, an extraordinarily successful businessman who had branched out into network marketing and built downlines in the tens of thousands. Tom's the kind of guy you watch closely. He has a golden touch, and when he called to invite me to join his organization, I listened carefully. Tom, it turned out, had just signed on as one of the very first distributors for a new, up-and-coming company that carried a line of unique health products. I knew the opportunity had to be big if he was involved, but I had learned my lesson about trying to work two businesses simultaneously. Besides, I was close to retiring from my present company. In other words, I had almost reached the level where I could receive substantial commissions without having to work the business full time. I didn't want to jeopardize that. Nonetheless, Usa and I signed on. We wanted to sample the products. If we liked them, well, maybe we'd just wholesale them. As Usa mentioned, she fell in love with the products, and the rest is history.

There was another reason I didn't jump into this new company. As a student of success, I wanted to learn more about how the industry's top earners reached the top. What did they know that the rest of us didn't? And so I returned to "school," reading profiles of these individuals in network marketing magazines, books and publications. I also called many of them and asked straight out for their secrets. As you'd expect from network marketers, they were friendly, helpful and enthusiastic. They told me much that, coupled with my own experiences, I've incorporated into *The 21-Day Challenge*. Speaking of which ... isn't it time you met Challenge #3?

Today's challenge

Go to the library or a bookstore, and meet the individuals who will be become your role models. For me, they were James Allen, Dale Carnegie, Dr. Norman Vincent Peale, Napoleon Hill and Maxwell Maltz, among others. The shelves are full of yet others, many of whom you'll find in the bibliography on Pages 103–106.

Don't get overwhelmed, however. Start with a single book and chapter. As you read, commit to finding one piece of information you can put to immediate use. Absorb it fully, then move on to the next piece. Here are a couple of great books to get you started: *Awaken the Giant Within: How to take immediate control of your mental, emotional, physical and financial destiny* by Anthony Robbins, and *Feel the Fear and Do It Anyway* by Susan Jeffers, Ph.D.

Challenge #3
Pinpoint your dreams

Presented by Usa*

What do you want in life? Wealth? Health? Happiness? Any and all can be yours — if you create a compelling enough vision of your future. For example, a few short years ago, I was working back-to-back shifts in two different fast-food restaurants, and still struggling to get by. My idea of financial well-being? To one day work a single shift and enjoy an occasional two-day weekend. Hardly a compelling vision.

But then my life took an incredible turn. I was introduced to network marketing. Suddenly, my idea of wealth changed; it became more specific. Witnessing firsthand the incredible success of my sponsor and other distributors, I drew up a long, detailed list of what true wealth meant to me.

My list revealed that I was no longer interested in making a good living; I wanted to create a phenomenal life instead. Sure, money was an important part of the picture, but so was building an exciting and strong business, and having time to enjoy the simple pleasures of life. And so I created a five-year plan for myself, with specific goals and rewards broken down by what I call life categories: professional/business, personal growth/relationships, income/material possessions and other. These goals and rewards have worked like a magnet, drawing me forward and keeping me going, even when I hit occasional walls. Best of all, they've allowed

---

* When it comes to presenting these Challenges, the two of us will sometimes take turns. In such situations, you'll find "Presented by Usa" or "Presented by Russ."

me to achieve ultimate success: the ability to share my blessings with others through Fuen-Surapee Boonyaparutayus Foundation, the charitable foundation I created to serve the needy in my native country, Thailand. I tell you this not to boast, but to share a conviction — that the greater your ability to envision the perfect life, the greater your ability to achieve it.

Today's challenge

So what is it that you want for yourself? Your family? How can network marketing help you realize your dreams? Be specific! Imagine yourself five years from now. How has your everyday life changed? What does it feel like to be your own boss? To control your time and destiny? To enjoy all of the big and little things life offers? Don't just think about the answers to these questions — see them, feel them. Make them part of you!

To facilitate the goal-setting process, group your goals into the following categories:

- Income
- Professional development
- Personal growth and relationships
- Physical well-being

Next, identify what you most want to achieve in each category at specific intervals (e.g., three months, six months, one year, three years, five years, etc.). Be ambitious, but realistic. For example, your goal may be to make a six-figure income and own a vacation home. Ambitious, yes. Realistic, maybe. It all depends on whether you aim to achieve your goal in two months or two years.

The very act of listing your goals and creating a timetable for their achievement increases your chances of success. This was proven by a Harvard University study that followed a group of graduates over the course of many years. The 3 percent of graduates who had set identifiable goals achieved their dreams. The remaining 97 percent fell short.

Suggested readings: Great books and tapes on goal-setting abound. Here are three: *Goals: How to Get Everything You Want — Faster Than You Thought Possible* by Brian Tracy; *Goals: Setting and Achieving Them on Schedule* by Zig Ziglar; and *First Things First* by Stephen R. Covey. I also suggest you read up on how to use visualization and affirmation to attract the results you want. One of my favorite books on the subject is Shakti Gawain's classic, *Creative Visualization: Use the power of your imagination to create what you want in your life.*

Challenge #4
Commit to your success

Presented by Usa

Each day, people around the world are drawn to the promise of network marketing, and each day, scores of others walk away, disillusioned. Why? What makes their experience so different from those who stand their ground and achieve incredible success? I have thought long and hard about this, and here's my conclusion: You've got to give in order to receive.

Network marketing may be a unique business model, but like all businesses, it works only if you do. No matter what product you sell or what company you join, you need to be the engine that drives your success. Unfortunately, too many people are content to be passengers. No wonder, then, that they're disappointed with the results of their effort — or should I say lack of effort?

Don't be that kind of person. Instead, commit to your own success. I made that commitment and look where I am today.

Was it easy? Yes ... and no. Let me explain.

Remember the saying "It takes years to become an overnight sensation"? Well, the same holds true for network marketing. There's so much to learn — about the system, the products and how (and how not) to approach prospects. There's also much to learn about yourself. All these things take time, lots of it. And they take effort. Lots of that, too.

When I finally found the right company for me, I was willing to give everything I had to the business. That meant working days, nights and weekends, calling friends of friends, attending meeting after meeting, and reading and talking to everyone I could to increase my knowledge and confidence. It was hard work, but it paid off.

Are *you* willing to give your business your all? Just saying yes is not enough. You must be willing to commit.

Today's challenge

In your notebook, block out times for prospecting, hosting home meetings, working with your sponsor and downline, and learning all you can about the industry, various companies and the products they offer. At the end of each day, jot down the actual time you've spent on these activities. Total your hours at the end of your week to assess your level of commitment. Are the hours sufficient to jump-start and/or sustain your network marketing career? If yes, great. If not, identify the areas that require more of your time and effort.

Remember:

- Action is commitment set in motion.
- Motion builds momentum.
- Momentum, over time, leads to success.

Suggested readings: It's hard to commit when you don't fully understand what you're committing to. That's why I recommend *Your First Year in Network Marketing* by Mark Yarnell and Rene Reid Yarnell. It provides a great overview of what's in store over the next 12 months and offers solid tips for keeping on track. I also suggest you brush up on your time management and organizational skills. You can't be all over the place if you want to get somewhere specific. Therefore, take a peek at books like the following: *Time Management for Unmanageable People* by Ann McGee-Cooper; *Organizing for Dummies* by Eileen Roth; and *Clutter's Last Stand: It's time to de-junk your life!* by Don Aslett.

Challenge #5

Become an expert

Presented by Russ

As you undoubtedly know, network marketing is a system for marketing and distributing goods and services. These goods and services can be anything from makeup, nutritional products and water filter systems, to pet products, computers and legal services.

Like other businesses, network marketing companies provide consumers with what they want and need. Their structure is unique, however. They don't have to go through middlemen to get their products into the hands of customers. Rather, they produce, market and distribute their goods directly to end users through distributors. Distributors are independent company representatives. They get a commission on every sale made. The more sales they make, the greater their profits.

And there you have it: network marketing in a nutshell. Before you walk away, however, thinking you know enough, let me assure you, you don't. You haven't even skimmed the surface. If you don't go deeper, you won't be able to explain the business to others, let alone bring them on board.

It's imperative, therefore, that you become as much of an expert as you can. You don't have to know about every company out there or their compensation structures (Stairstep, Breakaway, Matrix, Unilevel and their hybrids). But you should have a sense of who's doing what and how. How else will you assess the competition and identify the opportunity that's perfect for you?

You also should have a sense of just how hot the network marketing industry has become. Did you know, for example, that business pundits consider it one of the most exciting opportunities of the 21st century, and that the number of marketers worldwide has increased by about 300 percent in the last decade alone? Did you know that many network marketing companies are being traded on NASDAQ and the New York and American stock exchanges, or that traditional companies are adopting the industry model to extend their reach and increase their sales? This is all great news, and you should share it with prospects so they, too, can get excited. First, of course, you have to know what we're talking about.

Today's challenge

Become more knowledgeable about this great industry of ours. Read any and all books you can on how network marketing *really* works. Subscribe to an industry publication or to an e-newsletter that keeps abreast of industry trends. Visit the Web sites of various companies to see what they offer and how they operate. You also should speak with representatives from several companies to learn firsthand about their specific products and compensation plans.

Suggested readings: You'll get a great overview of network marketing in our book *Absolutely* Everything *You Need to Know About Prospecting*. Part 2, "Building Your Foundation," will be particularly helpful.* Additional information can be found in Keith Laggos' comprehensive textbook *Direct Sales: An overview.* And don't forget Richard Poe's *Wave 3: The new era in network marketing,* which profiles successful marketers from scores of different companies.

---

* For *information about ordering copies of* Absolutely *Everything* You Need to Know About Prospecting, *turn to the last page of this book.*

Challenge #6
Become a myth-buster

Presented by Russ

Not everyone knows a great thing when they see it. Some people need to see it again, and again. Perhaps they think it's too good to be true or that they're not good enough for it. Whatever the case, these individuals need to be reassured and educated. Prospects are the same way. Sure, you'll find some who are interested in network marketing in general, and your company in particular. Most, however, will be cautious, even skeptical.

As a distributor, it is your job to respond to your prospects' concerns and counter any misconceptions they may have. Generally, these objections can be grouped into what we call the seven myths of network marketing. We summarize the myths below and offer counter arguments for each.

Myth 1 — Network marketing is a pyramid scheme. This is one of the most common and inaccurate myths of all. One of your first orders of business, therefore, will be to draw a distinction between network marketing and pyramids.

Your prospects need to know that pyramid schemes are illegal. Legitimate network marketing companies, by contrast, offer quality goods and services at reasonable prices. These offerings are at the very heart of their business. In fact, they *are* the business. You don't have to be a distributor to purchase them, although you may opt to do so. Many individuals, in fact, take this route because it lets them buy products wholesale. They can then sell them retail and/or build a business by helping others do the same.

Myth 2 — No one gets rich in network marketing. Another falsehood. The industry is full of rags-to-riches stories and individuals who earn six- and seven-figure incomes. We should know — we're among them. The industry is also full of what we call nice-clothes-to-riches stories, namely, individuals who have left decent jobs and salaries behind to achieve greater wealth and independence. All prospects want to know if they will be among these ranks. The answer: It's up to you. If you work hard and persevere, you can make it.

Nonetheless, only 5 percent of all network marketers reach the upper echelons, and typically after some 10 years in the business. Ninety percent drop out by the end of their second year. Undoubtedly, your prospects will want to know what separates the top earners from the vast majority of others. The answers are simple: Wildly successful marketers are deeply committed to their companies and the network marketing model. They choose their companies wisely and work for one company only, as opposed to working for several simultaneously. They are also dynamic leaders who use vision, smarts and generosity of spirit to help others reach their personal and financial goals.

Myth 3 — It takes money to make money. Yes, it does, and don't let prospects think otherwise. Any and all network marketing companies have a startup fee that allows distributors to come into the business at the ground level. The fees themselves can range from $25–$1,000-plus. We believe that's reasonable, even cheap, considering the startup fees for other businesses

Are there costs beyond startup fees? Of course. Using the analogy of a clothing store, the suits and dresses don't come free, however, they can be purchased at reduced rates, allowing prospects to make a profit. Further, network marketers don't have to carry an inventory, track their sales or commissions, or pay to produce promotional materials. Their company assumes all of those costs.

Myth 4 — *You can become an overnight success.* We disagree. Our experience has shown that it takes a whole lot of days to become an overnight success. The network marketing model may be simple, but that doesn't mean any of us achieve success in a night, a week, a month or even a year. We certainly didn't. Rather, we worked long and hard for it. There wasn't a day when we didn't make at least a couple prospecting calls. There wasn't a week when we didn't host, or help others host, a home meeting. Even now, we keep working to build our business, though we do it part time ... most of the time, that is. Some months we work 12-hour days, not including the time Usa spends in Thailand, her native country, where she's spreading the word about network marketing and supporting her growing downline.

Myth 5 — *You need a downline of thousands to make money.* Distributors who stick with network marketing will one day have a downline of hundreds or even thousands. As you'll inform your prospects, it's part of the business model and one of the most exciting things about the industry. Imagine: They can work their own hours, all from home, and you can have a workforce of many dedicated individuals.

Nonetheless, your prospects should know they don't need all of these people to achieve success. All they need are one to three individuals. These are what we call the "golden nuggets," and you'll learn more about them in Challenge #9, "Cultivate Winners."

Myth 6 — *You've got to strong-arm people into signing up.*
Absolutely not! In fact, you must tell your prospects that doing so will have the opposite effect. They'll wind up recruiting people who joined only because they felt pressured to. The vast majority of these individuals will drop out by the end of their third week — and they'll blame their sponsors for their failure.

Accordingly, let prospects know that the soft sell is the best sell. It's the only sell. There's no need to strong-arm anyone. If you love your company and its products and services, if you believe in network marketing and all that it offers, you won't have to convince anyone of anything — you merely have to share what you believe to be a winning business opportunity. Not everyone will hear the call. Concentrate your efforts on those who do. Most prospects will understand and be relieved by this.

Myth 7 — You need to be a natural-born salesperson. How untrue! Just ask people who know the two of us, especially Usa. They'll tell you she's the shy, quiet type — and they're right. She still finds it hard to talk in front of groups of people, be they small or large. But what she may lack in courage, she makes up for in belief. She believes in network marketing, her company's products, her downline and, just as importantly, herself. Her sincerity shines through; it's what helped her grow her business.

Your prospects need to know that there are hundreds of thousands, maybe millions, of network marketers out there like her. We've recruited quite a few of them ourselves and continue to be amazed at how effective the shy, silent types can be. Their contributions prove that network marketing truly is the great equalizer — not just financially, but personally. It allows people of all races, creeds, colors and backgrounds to achieve success, just as it allows people of various personality types to realize their dreams.

Today's challenge

Familiarize yourself with each of the seven myths. You will have to debunk each and every one at some point while prospecting. Formulate and practice your responses, so you can speak with confidence. Be straightforward and sincere in your delivery.

Suggested readings: A must-read for all in our profession is the ground-breaking work of Charles King, Ph.D., professor of marketing at the University of Illinois at Chicago. In his book, *The New Professionals: The rise of network marketing as the next Major profession,* Dr. King presents industry statistics and trends that support the industry's projected growth and its legitimacy. This information does much to dispel the myths surrounding network marketing.

Challenge #7
Fall in love with your company and products

Presented by Usa

As I mentioned in Challenge #1, I stumbled upon the network marketing company for which I am now an independent distributor. Actually, I should say it stumbled upon me. Russ and I were already with another company, and it was almost as an afterthought that I sampled its products. Within a few days, I experienced a greater sense of physical well-being and energy. Pleasant surprise though this was, it wasn't until friends also sampled the products and gave them an enthusiastic thumbs-up that I examined the company's line more closely. I not only liked what I saw, I loved it.

I share this information, not to pitch my company but to make an important point: You've got to fall head over heels in love with your product. As obvious as that may seem, too few network marketers do. They'll sell anything to anyone if it makes them money. No wonder they fail. Prospects and customers see through the act and steer clear. It's a lose-lose proposition all the way around.

Loving your products allows you to speak with a sincere and infectious enthusiasm. But for that enthusiasm to last, you also have to fall in love with your company.

Network marketing companies are not all alike. Some are simply better than others in terms of products, support and compensation plans. That's why it's critical that you make a smart choice.

Know what you're getting into. Is the company you're considering legitimate? Are its products unique, competitively priced and of high quality? Do they have mass, sustainable appeal? In other words, will people want to purchase them today as well as tomorrow? Flash-in-the-pan products are made by flash-in-the-pan com-

49

panies — the very ones you want to avoid.

What do you know about the company's management? Are its officers experienced industry veterans? How has the company performed under their "watch"? What kind of compensation plan does the company offer? When and how are commission checks paid? What incentives does the company offer its distributors? Bonuses? Trips to exotic locations? Free luxury cars?

As you can see, you have some homework to do, but it will be well worth your effort. To this, I can personally attest.

Today's challenge

Contact several companies for comparison purposes. Study their promotional materials. Visit their Web sites. Watch their videos. Listen to their audiotapes. Attend a home meeting. Order a sample kit to give you a more intimate sense of what the company and its products are all about.

Try the company's products over the course of a few days or even weeks, so you can decide for yourself whether the products live up to their promises. If possible, have family and friends also sample the goods. Their feedback will help you make a more objective decision.

Suggested readings: To learn more about choosing the network marketing company that's right for you, consult Pages 63–65 of our book *Absolutely* Everything *You Need to Know About Prospecting.* This information is critical if you're to make a smart decision.

Week 2

8. Follow the leader

9. Cultivate winners

10. Compile your warm list

11. Warm up to cold calls

12. Go retail

13. Work your list

14. Create a winning presentation

Challenge #8
Follow the leader

Presented by Usa

As an independent distributor, you're in great company. There are hundreds, thousands, perhaps even millions of "yous" out there, depending on your company. But don't worry about the competition. As mentioned in Challenge #5, "Become an expert," the network marketing industry is exploding. Between 1990 and 2000, for example, network marketing sales doubled, from $13 billion to $26 billion. Imagine what they are today!

To tap into this revolution, it's critical to follow the marketing system established by your company. After all, network marketing is first and foremost a system — a system for success. Although you may be new to the business, the business itself is highly evolved. All policies and procedures have been worked out to a science. That means you don't have to reinvent the wheel or waste your time and energy on the countless details that plague most other startups (e.g., employee recordkeeping, bookkeeping and advertising). Rather, by following your company's blueprint for success, you have the freedom to grow your business quickly and efficiently, and to enjoy the financial rewards that much sooner.

Unfortunately, not all new distributors get off to a great start. Far too many stumble or drop out within a relatively short time. And the reason is simple: They deviate from the system. I know of no bigger mistake you can make.

These words may be hard to swallow. A part of you may well be insisting: "But I'm an individual. I want to do things my way." Understand that you're not being asked to be someone you're not. You are, however, being asked to follow a set system. And for good reason: It works.

Change course and you'll get lost, plus you'll confuse your downline. Neither you nor they will know what to do next or why, let alone what results to expect. That's no way to run a business.

Once you've mastered the basics, you can —in fact, you should — experiment with different marketing techniques to build your downline. That's where creativity and personal style come into play, for, ultimately, you're your best marketing tool.

Today's challenge

Become intimately familiar with your company's training materials, such as tapes, CDs and videos. Sign up for any teleconferences or conventions you can. And don't forget to surf your company's Web site. It will keep you abreast of the latest developments: new products, markets, bonus systems and the like. Block out time to do this *today*.

Suggested readings: There's more than one way to follow more than one leader. One of my "leaders" is Robert T. Kiyosaki, author of the phenomenal best-seller *Rich Dad, Poor Dad*. One of his more recent books is also worth reading: *The Business School for People Who Like Helping People: The eight hidden values of a network marketing business, other than making money.* (Cashflow). In it, he presents his "CASHFLOW Quadrant," which outlines the key to long-term prosperity. He's made a believer — and a follower — out of me!

Challenge #9
Cultivate winners

Presented by Usa

Network marketing is a people business. That's what makes it unique and fun. Every day is different, filled with people who can help you grow your business in large and small ways. Cultivate them. This is especially important when it comes to the key individuals in your upline.

Develop a strong relationship with your sponsor. She has walked the same road you're now on, so why not turn to her for advice and direction? He has experienced your same fears and insecurities, so why not let him share his techniques for moving past them?

For example, when I decided to branch out on my own and become an independent distributor for my present company, I followed the lead of my sponsor. As I mentioned in Challenge #1, he was a veteran marketer who had worked with several companies over the years, building a downline of thousands and drawing a million-dollar income. I knew that he walked the talk. I was only too happy to learn all I could from him.

Your sponsor, like mine, is part teacher, part guide, part cheerleader, part friend. That's a whole lot of parts! And when you put them together, you get an energetic, knowledgeable and caring person who will help you get where you want to go as directly as possible.

Know, however, that your upline includes more than just your sponsor. Your sponsor's sponsor (or even your sponsor's sponsor's sponsor) is someone with helpful tools and tips. Don't be shy about giving him a quick phone call or dropping her an e-mail. Expand your reach and knowledge. Sure, it may be a bit scary to approach someone you don't know well, or at all, especially someone you've admired from a distance. But don't forget: You're members of the same family — namely, your company. What supports one member ultimately supports all.

It's also important to work closely with the winners in your downline. As Russ mentioned in Challenge #6, "Become a myth-buster,"* you don't have to have a downline of thousands. What you *do* need is a handful of distributors who have heard the calling and responded body and soul. These individuals understand the unique, high-quality products you represent, and they're genuinely excited by the business opportunities their cutting-edge company offers. These are the distributors you should cultivate.

Because cultivation takes time, you must use it wisely. You don't want to put endless energy into getting all of your new distributors charged up, for example. Sure, cheerleading is important (heck, I still need it!), but it can only go so far. Distributors have to go the rest of the way themselves. If they're reluctant, no amount of pushing or pulling will change their minds or the way they do business. Their businesses won't grow, period.

So why put your energies into a losing proposition? Instead, concentrate on your winners: the core group of distributors like you who understand that their company is not just a business but a way of life. Although they may be few in number, they can — indeed, they will — be incredibly effective in building your organization. Stay in close touch with them. Help them set and reach their goals. Be there when they need advice, support or a sounding board. Let them know how much you care so, together, you can become a winning team.

---

* See Page 43.

Today's challenge

Today's challenge is twofold. First, identify a successful individual in your upline. Schedule a time to talk shop, be it in person or by phone or e-mail. Ask him (or her) to share any suggestions he may have for helping you build a business as successful as his. Once you've spoken with this person, identify a second, then a third, etc.

My second suggestion is to make it a point of being available to the winners in your downline. Don't let this responsibility scare you. Thanks to Challenge #8, "Follow the leader," you've already become a master follower and are now ready to lead. Expect to feel like a novice at times, but that's a good thing. It means you're putting yourself out there, forging new ground and mastering new knowledge areas. You will become the winner they want to emulate.

Suggested readings: We've mentioned several great books on network marketing in previous Challenges. To this illustrious group, we'd like to add two more: Richard Poe's *Wave 4: Network marketing in the 21st century* and Randy Gage's *How to Build a Multi-level Marketing Machine.* Both present practical information on how to bring the best and brightest people into your organization.

Challenge #10
Compile your warm list

Presented by Russ

Prospects come in all shapes and sizes, ages and backgrounds. No wonder there's no one way to approach them all. What works for you may not work for them. That's why I believe in balancing warm and cold calls — and adding retailing to the mix. Used together, they will strengthen your presentation skills and increase your prospect pool. In today's Challenge, we'll concentrate on warm calls.

Warm calls are just that — calls you make to individuals who may be responsive to your products, services and/or business opportunity. Note the word *may*. Just because you know someone doesn't guarantee anything. All it means is that you're more likely to get an audience.

Be inclusive, not exclusive, when compiling your list. Don't make assumptions about who would or wouldn't make a good prospect. For example, don't assume that someone without a college degree won't recognize a great opportunity, or that someone in her late 60s won't have the drive to grow a solid business. Don't assume that a successful CEO won't be interested in starting from the bottom, or that a mother of five has no time to earn extra income. Remember, network marketing is the great equalizer. Give everyone an equal chance.

Some of the industry's top earners believe you should never, ever cross a prospect off your list, even if he or she goes from warm to cold. Circumstances change and so do minds, they maintain. Someone uninterested in becoming a distributor one day may become interested the following week, month or year. Perhaps he's just retired or been laid off from work; perhaps she wants to switch careers or supplement her family's income. I agree, but I also agree with other network marketers who suggest you purge from your list all prospects clearly cool to your company, its products or the network marketing model in general. Sure, you should give them the benefit of the doubt by following up several times, but if they still don't hear the call, you should consider putting your energies into finding those who do.*

So where does all this leave you? Somewhere in the middle, and that's just fine. Our experience shows that it's good business practice to close the door on some prospects and keep it open for others. We have no set formula for making these decisions; we just use the sixth sense we've developed over the years. You'll develop this sense too.

One final note regarding warm prospects — don't expect any or all of them to sign up immediately. None may sign up at all. Difficult as this may be to accept, it's their prerogative. Don't try to force the issue or lay on the guilt. Move on. You wouldn't want them as distributors anyway.

---

* There is one group of prospects we never, ever, take off our lists — veteran network marketers. As we discuss in Challenge #18, "Enlist vets," these people already understand and believe in the business model. More importantly, they are always open to new opportunities. Present the right one to them, and they'll not only join your organization but bring their downlines with them. Don't expect this to happen after one or two phone calls over the course of a few months, however. Our experience shows that you sometimes have to stay in touch with them for years, maybe even decades. This was borne out recently when a vet joined Usa's company after 36 years with another company. And guess who came along with him? All 35,000-plus of his distributors!

Today's challenge

Get started on compiling your warm list by identifying 10 individuals who would be open to hearing about your products and/or business opportunity. Next, group them into categories. For example, as you look over your list, note those individuals who would be most interested in earning extra income, in changing careers, in purchasing products, etc. This allows you to approach one group at a time, which has two advantages: 1) You'll develop a repertoire of presentations, polishing each one as you go along; and 2) It becomes easier to respond to prospects' questions and concerns, and to follow up with targeted phone calls and materials.

Suggested readings: If you'd like to learn how to prospect for gold in your own backyard, read Chapter 4 of our book *Absolutely Everything You Need to Know About Prospecting*. We also suggest you read Kim Klaver's *The Truth: What it really takes to make it in network marketing*, an irreverent look at the kinds of people you should — and shouldn't — recruit. And don't forget Mark Yarnell's *Your Best Year in Network Marketing: How to achieve the financial success you deserve*. We particularly like his "Warm Memory Jogger" on Pages 48–51.

Challenge #11
Warm up to cold calls

Cold calls. What an awful expression! And what images it conjures up! You imagine your heart stopping cold. You can almost feel yourself shiver inside. You fear your words will freeze in midair, that your prospect will give you a chilly response, an icy stare.

We hate to admit it, but these are legitimate concerns — but that doesn't mean you shouldn't cold call or that only warm calls guarantee results. A warm lead may well be a cold lead if the person you're approaching has zip interest in your business opportunity. Accordingly, it's important to use both approaches.

We certainly do. For example, while we're in line at the post office or exercising in the gym, we make a point of socializing with others. Should they seem open to new ideas, we tell them about how we built a profitable home-based business working part time. Often they want to hear more, and so we tell them. Before we part, we hand them a business card and ask if we can send them an informational packet. We assure them we're not trying to sell them anything; rather, we only want to share an opportunity. As you can see, this kind of cold call can quickly become a warm call. Had we restricted our efforts to making only warm calls, we would have missed important leads.

Cold calling can take other forms. Among them: distributing fliers and business cards in well-traveled places; placing ads in magazines, newspapers and community freebies; making presentations at professional associations, church groups, parents' groups, etc.; and renting facilities for conducting large-scale opportunity meetings. The list goes on.

Are these efforts worth the time and money? Many successful

network marketers would say no. Make that a resounding no. They believe you should limit your activities to approaches that have a greater likelihood of success. We tend to agree and yet ... you might get lucky. As mentioned in Challenge #9, "Cultivate winners," you don't need to recruit thousands to have a downline of thousands. All you need is a handful of committed individuals. You may well find one or two of them through cold calling.

Here's another reason to incorporate cold calling in your repertoire: Cold contacts are limitless, while warm contacts may cool with time. This happens when you exhaust (but only temporarily!) the list of prospects you know well. You must then get referrals from personal contacts. Many of these will be cold calls.

Today's challenge

Make a list of hot spots for making cold calls (e.g., church functions, cocktail parties, community meetings, etc.). Seek out opportunities for striking up conversations with acquaintances or strangers while in these environments. No heavy selling, however! You're simply testing the waters.

Put together packets of promotional materials and product samples to carry with you or stash in your car. This way, you have something to distribute to interested individuals, paving the way for future contacts.

Suggested readings: In Chapter 4 of our book *Absolutely Everything You Need to Know About Prospecting,* you'll get hot tips for developing your cold list. We also suggest that you read the classic, *Cold Calling Techniques (That Really Work!)* by Stephen Schiffman. Finally, it's important for you to create an "elevator speech" that lets prospects know who you are and what you do in seconds. You'll get the pointers you need in *How to Write a Compelling 30-Second Commercial of Yourself* by Debra Koontz Traverso.

Challenge #12
Go retail

Warm calls, cold calls. As discussed, we need to do both if we're to expand our organizations. We also need to retail our products if we're to put ourselves in the big leagues.

There are several reasons for this. First, retailing creates a loyal customer base and repeat business. Happy customers spread the word, recruiting others in the process. In essence, they prospect for you.

Second, retailing is itself a powerful prospecting tool. You don't have to convince customers of anything; they're already converts. They know your company is credible and have experienced its growth firsthand. They even know how to sell products to others based on your example. This makes it much easier to take them to the next level, namely, to becoming distributors.

Third, retailing can build your business more quickly, especially if you're more comfortable selling products than a business opportunity.

Fourth, retailing provides a regular source of income. Depending on your circumstances, this may well be enough to meet your financial needs. Retail sales do more than that, however. In fact, they can help you build an enormously profitable business. That's because they build your personal group volume, making you eligible for company discounts, bonuses and other incentives. The same holds true for your customers. The more they sell, the more they make, and the greater their incentive to increase their volume or become distributors themselves. A major selling point for retailing then is that you need to recruit fewer individuals. If you get your customers to sell five times the minimum volume, you'll need only one-tenth the number of people in your downline.

Fifth, retailing keeps you on the up and up. If your focus is on recruiting distributors rather than on selling products, you're doing your company and network marketing a disservice. The industry has fought long and hard for legitimacy. Don't blow it. Quality products and services should — indeed must — be at the heart of all that you do.

Today's challenge

With the above in mind, review your warm list and identify prospects who'd make great customers. Think, too, of ways cold-calling techniques could be used to expand retail sales.

Suggested readings: For more detail about how to use retail to build your business, read Chapter 4 of *Absolutely* Everything *You Need to Know About Prospecting*. We also suggest that you brush up on your conversational skills, as interpersonal relationships are critical to selling. One of our favorite books along these lines is *The Confident Schmoozer* by Beth Mende Conny. Within it you'll find great insights into how you can build on your strengths, move beyond your fears and better anticipate what others want.

Challenge #13
Work your list

Presented by Russ

While having a long list of leads is great, it doesn't get you anywhere if you don't work it. After all, a name on a piece of paper is just a bunch of letters, nothing more than a missed opportunity.

On the day I began working with my company, I promised myself I would approach at least two prospects a day. I was given this advice by the No. 1 earner in my company, and it has guided me ever since. In fact, I credit much of my success to that one suggestion.

Two contacts a day equals 730 prospects a year.* Out of that number, I have found the nuggets of gold who have helped build my organization. I suggest that you commit to this approach, too.

Making this commitment is serious business, which is how it should be. Prospecting haphazardly or only when you feel like it doesn't cut it, not if you're determined to achieve lifelong prosperity. If achieving prosperity is not your aim, you're in the wrong business.

I know how difficult, and even scary, it can be to identify two individuals, let alone set up meetings with them. I've been there, done that. Nevertheless I know — and I promise — that it gets easier. Remember, success is a muscle that you build over time. With each success you get stronger, and meeting with two people a day becomes less daunting.

Although this technique has worked so well for me, it may not be the best for you. Lifestyle, responsibilities, schedule — all will

---

By the way, these contacts don't necessarily have to be in person. Meetings by phone also count — as long as they're serious calls, meaning those in which you discuss your business opportunity rather than shoot the breeze.

influence when and how you prospect. Some network marketers, for example, make their prospecting calls on weekends only. Others go full throttle for a solid week a month. Whatever works for you, works.

Nonetheless, it's important to set goals for yourself. Be ambitious but realistic about the number of contacts you will make. Whatever you do, don't make calls just to say you've made them. Quality, not quantity, counts. Racing through a dozen calls won't increase your chances of recruiting distributors, but it might well ruin them. Prospects know when someone is using them, and they'll turn off immediately. What a waste. The whole point of prospecting is to turn people on.

Goals are important for yet another reason: They help you see beyond the present. As you may or may not know, about 70 percent of distributors give up after the first three weeks. Expecting overnight success, they quickly become frustrated. Rather than continuing to work their lists, they make fewer and fewer contacts, until they have all but guaranteed their failure.

Another reason these new marketers fail is because they don't follow up. Follow-ups are an inevitable part of the prospecting process, however. Serious prospects need time to assess their level of commitment, study a company's products and compensation plan, and consult with their significant others. They'll have questions to be answered, concerns to be addressed.

If possible, set up a time to get back in touch with prospects, be it by phone or in person, one week or one month down the road. Do this before the end of your first one-on-one or home meeting, so you both know what's to happen next. This gives you an important "in" when you do make contact. You can then say something like: "Marsha, hi. This is Bob Casey of XYZ. Thanks again for coming to the get-together (home meeting) at Larry's last week. I'm calling today at your suggestion, to follow up on your interest in becoming a distributor."

Should prospects be too busy to talk or seem uninterested at the time of your follow-up, don't give up. Their response may have little to do with you and everything to do with what's going on in their lives. Perhaps they're in the midst of a work deadline or their children have chickenpox. Perhaps you simply called at the wrong time — too early or late in the day. Don't assume the worst. Rather, set up another time to talk. Let them know you're available in the meantime, and provide them with your contact information (e.g., phone and fax numbers, snail mail and e-mail addresses).

Call or drop prospects a line thanking them for meeting with you. If you promised to send promotional materials or samples, do so immediately. It's critical that you keep your word. You must strike while the iron is hot. The more time that passes between your initial and subsequent contacts, the greater the likelihood that prospects will forget who you are and what you shared.

Finally — and this should go without saying — it's important to make note of all information garnered through your interchanges. We're talking about more than name, rank and serial number here. Rather, focus on personal data, such as where individuals live and work, what they most want from network marketing (to launch a new career, supplement present income, work from home), their marital status and personal interests, etc. These details should be noted in writing to jog your memory, for just as prospects may have poor retention over time, so might you. You need key information at your disposal if you are to continue to build a meaningful relationship with prospects. How else can you demonstrate that you remember them and care?

Today's challenge

Set realistic but ambitious prospecting goals for yourself. How many calls will you do a day? A minimum of two or five? If you don't set a daily quota, how about a weekly one? How many contacts will you commit to making by week's end or over the course of a month? Be specific. Write this number down in your journal and create a system for assessing how well you met your goals.

Suggested readings: Follow-up is critical, which is why we recommend reading Chapter 5 of *Absolutely* Everything *You Need to Know About Prospecting.* We also suggest that you investigate some of the many great books on building strong relationships with customers. Here's a title to start with: *The Customer Driven Company: Moving from talk to action* by Richard C. Whiteley.

Challenge #14
Create a winning presentation

An effective presentation, be it for a home or one-on-one meeting, is one that opens the door to new distributors and customers. Note that we said *opens the door*. No matter how much you may wish to, you can't force anyone to walk through it.

Prospects will pass on your offer for various reasons, many of which may have little to do with you. But take heed: Just because someone leaves your meeting uncommitted or seemingly turned off doesn't mean he or she isn't interested. You may well have planted a seed that flowers several weeks or months later. That's all the more reason to prepare a polished and compelling presentation.

When you speak, do so in terms of benefits. Your prospects aren't meeting with you to hear your success story. They want to know how they will achieve success, personally, professionally and financially.

Whatever you do, avoid false promises. They reflect badly on you, your company and the industry. Further, they do nothing to build your business. Oh, you may get a few starry-eyed individuals who want to become distributors, but don't be fooled. They won't stay long. Besides, if your company, its products and compensation plan are as great as you say they are, there's no need for hype.

Although all presentations have the same components, the components themselves can be presented in any order. Some network marketers, for example, lead with their company's business opportunity, and then discuss products and services. Others lead with products and services, and then move on to compensation plans and the like. Whatever approach you choose, your presentation should include the following:

- Information about how network marketing works and what makes it a revolutionary form of doing business.

- An overview of your company and its unique, high-quality products and services.

- A brief but informative discussion of your company's compensation plan, illustrated in handouts or on a chart large enough for all to see.

- A promotional video and/or distribution of company brochures, starter kits, etc.

- A demonstration of retail products and distribution of samples.

- Testimonials from you, your sponsor and other distributors as to how the business opportunity worked for each of you (e.g., how you've tripled your income, now work part time, spend more time with your family, etc.).

- A question-and-answer period.

  Play with these elements to see what order works best for you.

Today's challenge

Create a presentation that incorporates the elements listed above. Try it out on friends and family, your colleagues and, more importantly, your sponsor. Be open to suggestions and make the necessary adjustments. Ask your sponsor to accompany you on your initial prospect calls and to co-host home meetings until you feel more comfortable. If possible, conduct three-way phone calls with your sponsor and prospects to learn yet other prospecting techniques.

Suggested readings: In *Absolutely* Everything *You Need to Know About Prospecting*, Chapter 5, "Going one-on-one," we offer other tips for creating a winning presentation. In that chapter, we also give you pointers on meeting logistics and ways to rein in "prospects from hell," namely, negative attention-seekers who threaten to disrupt an otherwise great gathering. We also suggest that you read any and all of the network marketing books we've mentioned previously. Each of them will have at least some information on how to structure your presentation for maximum effectiveness. Finally, you might want to read up on sales presentations in general. For example: *Power Sales Presentations: Complete sales dialogues for each critical step of the sales cycle* by Stephen Schiffman.

Week 3

15. Reject rejection

16. Expand your reach

17. Get Internet savvy

18. Enlist vets

19. Pick from the family tree

20. Network

21. Think positive

Challenge #15
Reject rejection

Presented by Usa

Before we move on to more advanced business-building techniques, let's pause to discuss one of the most difficult aspects of network marketing — rejection. Ours is a profession in which we get a lot more nos than yeses. This can be dispiriting, no matter how many years you've been at it. But don't take it personally. More often than not, a "no" has little to do with you. Let me use an analogy to illustrate my point.

Imagine it's a Friday night and you head off to a movie. You've heard somewhere (was it a movie review or a snippet of a conversation?) that the film you're about to see is great, a real blockbuster, and every word turns out to be true. Excitedly, you tell everyone you know about it — family, friends, neighbors, colleagues, even strangers. Some folks are so caught up in your enthusiasm that they run out to the theater. Of these, some will share your sentiments and others will be unimpressed. Other folks won't even go to the theater; their tastes simply differ or they have other things to do. Would you feel rejected by those who either didn't like the film or chose not to go? Of course not!

Film recommendations, network marketing ... if you really think about it, they're one and the same thing. You share an opportunity, wanting the best for others. It's then up to them to decide whether to take advantage of it. Ultimately, there is little you can do to affect the outcome.

You can, however, keep the following comforting ideas in mind:

Understand that a "no" is often a "not yet." Timing is everything in life and in network marketing. Often, individuals who say no really mean that they can't move forward at that moment; they have other work and family obligations that make it difficult, if not impossible, for them to proceed. That's why I always keep the names of such individuals on file. A few months down the line may make all the difference in the world.

Don't reject others in advance. In my first year of network marketing, it was especially easy to fall into the "assumption trap." That trap goes something like this: "Oh, I can't call him/her. He/she is too busy/important/wealthy/well-placed/educated/savvy, etc." In short, I'd reject prospects before they had a chance to reject me. That's a lose-lose situation for all.

Increase your odds by increasing your numbers. The greater the number of prospects you approach, the greater your chances of finding the handful of people who can help you grow your business. So put the odds in your favor. Make your calls regularly.

Get support. Put your sponsor to work for you. It's no accident, after all, that you find the word "up" in upline. Let him or her lift your spirits, offer perspective and share tips and tools to increase your effectiveness. Remember: You're part of a winning team, so draw on the strength of others.

Today's challenge

Contact your sponsor to learn about strategies you can employ should you receive more nos than yeses. Another option is to contact other distributors and form a support group that meets regularly in person or by phone.

Suggested readings: To counter your fear of rejection, we have two great antidotes. Both are lovely, pocket-sized books whose titles say it all: *Believe in Yourself* and *Dare to Believe*, written by Beth Mende Conny. Here's are two other shot-in-the-arm titles: *The*

Ultimate Secret to Getting Absolutely Everything You Want by Mike Hernacki and *Feel the Fear ... and Beyond: Mastering the techniques of doing it anyway."* Written by Susan Jeffers, Ph.D., this book is a follow-up to her best-seller *Feel the Fear and Do It Anyway.*

Challenge #16
Expand your reach

Last week we devoted two of our Challenges to creating warm and cold lists. We don't know of any successful — or ultrasuccessful — network marketer who skipped either step when building their business. That said, lists are not enough. They shrink with time, as the number of meetings expands. Further, there's only so much of you to go around. Short of cloning yourself, you'll have to find other ways of extending your reach. We list some of these in this chapter.

All of these methods work, but not for everyone. Much depends on your goals, skills, budget and style. What works initially may not work later on, and vice versa. Nonetheless, we share these ideas to spark your thinking and doing. We also suggest that you try several approaches. As we've learned from experience, you increase your chances of success by working on more than one front.

- Sponsor local activities to gain visibility (e.g., a 5K run to benefit the library).

- Regularly thank steady customers for their business via coupons, special offers, etc.

- Link your products to special occasions (e.g., Mother's Day, Christmas, etc.).

- Distribute items featuring your company's name (e.g., pens, calendars, note pads).

- Turn your business card into a miniature billboard by using the reverse side to share information about yourself or your company.

- Turn your car into a moving advertisement using bumper stickers, window decals and magnetic signs.
- Pool resources with colleagues and conduct joint home and hall meetings.
- Teach an adult education class on network marketing or a topic related to your product.
- Write articles for local newspapers and magazines.
- Run classified or display ads in selected publications, or in coupon books and card decks.
- Place fliers in strategic locations.
- Use direct mail to announce a new product or business opportunity.
- Get an 800 number.
- Offer a teleconference to recruit distributors or train existing ones.

Today's challenge

Review the list above and identify those ideas that could work well for you, given your style, budget and goals. Choose just one to experiment with and develop an appropriate game plan. Once you've tackled that one, concentrate on another.

Suggested readings: In *Absolutely* Everything *You Need to Know About Prospecting,* we offer dozens of suggestions for marketing your business. You'll find Chapter 6, "Beyond the One-on-one," particularly helpful. We'd also like to recommend books like *303 Marketing Tips Guaranteed to Boost Your Business* by Rieva Lesonsky. This easy-to-read handbook comes to you from the publishers of *Entrepreneur* magazine. You can find good information in the *Idiot's guides* to marketing and to direct marketing. You can also investigate the *Dummies Guide to Marketing.*

Challenge #17
Get Internet savvy

Although one-on-one prospecting will always be at the heart of your efforts to build your network marketing business, the World Wide Web is changing the way we do business. It can be a power-house when it comes to increasing your exposure and reaching the 94 percent of the world's population who live outside the United States. Better yet, prospects worldwide will have a way to reach you 24 hours a day, seven days a week, 365 days a year. Even the most successful of network marketers can't put in those kind of hours! In that sense, the Internet can be a real money-maker. It allows you to extend your reach and thereby fast track your success. Hence, the importance of having your own Web site.

Everyone and their grandmother has a Web site, and we think you should too — if your site doesn't replicate that of your company. Consider this: All major network marketing companies have Web sites. They've paid big bucks to develop them, as they should. That's because Web sites are a necessity. All businesses today (let alone public and private institutions) are expected to have one. Those that do not are perceived as being behind the times. Worse, they lose out to the competition.

A comprehensive Web site makes a great first impression. Prospects have instant access to information about product lines, commission structures, customer and distributor support and other benefits. They can also learn about your company's officers, history and projected sales. Add video- and audioclips to the mix, and you have a site that does a whole lot of legwork for you at little cost.

But that's not all. Forward-thinking companies allow cus-tomers and distributors to order products and prospecting kits online. Many also serve as a Web host by offering their distributors free, personalized Web pages. If your company provides this service, take full advantage of it. It's certainly less expensive than creating your own site, and can only complement your other marketing efforts. Nonetheless, we believe you should at least consider launching a site of your own.

First of all, it's a more personal introduction to your company. In a sense, your site is an online version of a home meeting. You greet your guests at the door (your home page), make your presentation, and then answer their questions (via the links and content presented on your other pages).

Second, it's a relationship-builder. Your site does more than relay information. It presents a snapshot of who you are, sometimes literally.

Third, it's a showcase for your expertise. Your site can offer tips and tools on building a list, warming up to cold calls, growing your downline, etc. You can even gear your content to specific audiences (e.g., working mothers, retirees, professionals seeking new careers, etc.).

Fourth, it's a vehicle for spreading the news. Thanks to your site, prospects can learn where and when company meetings will be held. They can also keep abreast of new product lines, changes to your company's compensation plan, the industry's growth and consumer trends. You can also use your site as a classroom, making available materials distributors can use to strengthen their skills.

I could probably list 100 more reasons why Web sites are so helpful. Great as these sites may be, however, you can't assume that "if you build it, they will come." They won't, which is why you have to find other ways to promote yourself. The Internet offers scores of them. Usa and I introduce you to them in greater detail in *Absolutely* Everything *You Need to Know About Prospecting*, but I'll give you an abbreviated listing here. For example, you can:

- Publish articles, columns and nuggets of information and post them on sites other than your own. This gives you more visibility and increases the number of hits you get when people search for your name on, say, Google, Internet Explorer, etc.

- Place banner ads, which give you the No. 1 position on requested Web pages.

- Purchase pop-up or pop-under ads, which open on top of or beneath a Web page.

- Try "rich media" ads, which make use of video or animation. Like banner ads, they appear at the top of a Web page.

- Use click-through ads, which look and read like classified ads. Individuals who click on them are taken directly to the advertiser's site.

- Place classified ads at newsgroups and on bulletin boards.

- Launch an e-newsletter to build ongoing relationships and keep prospects in the loop. They should be mailed regularly to opt-in subscribers looking for timely and relevant information.

- Create an e-book readers can download in moments, one that tells readers more about you, your products and your business opportunity.

- Post on bulletin boards. Many are free; others have annual membership fees. Members use the service to share and receive information in keeping with their interests.

- Join discussion groups, which work much like bulletin boards in that they draw individuals with specific interests. Here, however, you post messages that other participants read and respond to. While you can't hawk a particular company, product or service, you can share this information indirectly.

- Chat online. Chat rooms are just that — online, real-time discussions in which individuals exchange text messages.

Finally, let's discuss direct marketing via e-mail. The upside of this approach is that it is considered effective even if it garners only a couple of new distributors. That's because it generally costs as much to send one piece of e-mail as it does to send thousands, or even millions. The downside is that such e-mail is increasingly being considered spam, even when individuals opt-in to receive it. The government has been working with Internet providers and software manufacturers to curb the flow of spam, which now accounts for more than half of all e-mail received daily. Accordingly, our enthusiasm for this marketing strategy has cooled.

Today's challenge

Undoubtedly, this Challenge has given you more information than you can use at this time, or perhaps even in a year from now. That's to be expected if you are new to the Internet. But take comfort — even Internet leaders and dedicated geeks are scrambling to keep up with this ever-changing technology. Therefore, I suggest you start with two things. First, just surf the Web to see what's out there. What do you like or find effective? If click-through ads or chat rooms hold no appeal, you should consider putting your efforts elsewhere.

The second thing I suggest is that you spend a half-hour navigating your company's Web site. Your company may well offer you your own free page to which your prospects can link. Should you want greater visibility and choose to launch your own site, make sure it complements, rather than duplicates or competes with, that of your company. Certainly, you should always "toe the company line." Never, ever, make false representations or promises.

Finally, spend time visiting other distributors' sites, be they in your company or those of its competitors. Identify what you like and don't like to better determine the design and graphic elements you want in your site. From there, you can begin to determine the costs associated with going online:

Suggested readings: Read *Absolutely* Everything *You Need to Know About Prospecting,* Chapter 7, "World Wide Web, Worldwide Reach," which goes into great detail about how you can use the Internet (not just Web pages) to build your business worldwide. Other great Internet marketing books abound, as a quick search on Amazon.com will reveal. Here are three we have found helpful: *Relationship Marketing on the Internet* by Roger C. Parker; *Guerrilla Marketing Online Weapons* by Jay Conrad Levinson and Charles Rubin; and *The 11 Immutable Laws of Internet Branding* by Al Ries and Laura Ries.

Challenge #18
Enlist vets

Presented by Russ

When you are new to the industry, your two most important jobs are to create and work your list of cold and warm leads. You have hundreds of ways to do so. Which you choose is up to you, for as Usa noted, personal style plays a factor. Nonetheless, you must keep at it. Lists, after all, last only so long. If you don't keep adding names to them, your business will stall, or, given attrition rates, will revert to an earlier, less profitable stage.

Veteran marketers also work their lists. But the smart ones — namely, the industry's top earners — do so strategically. They prospect *other network marketers*. As noted earlier, these prospects don't have to ramp up. They already have an intimate knowledge of the business and appreciate its great potential. Why else would they stay in the profession? That doesn't mean all of these prospects will pan out, however; only that the likelihood of this happening is greatly increased. We can personally attest to that.

Remember the stories of how Usa and I hooked up with our present companies? Both of us were approached by veterans, seemingly out of nowhere. The calls were not by chance, however. These individuals knew we were experienced marketers, even if we weren't particularly successful at that point. Accordingly, they didn't first have to sell us on the industry. They could concentrate instead on describing their business opportunities. It made the prospecting process easier and quicker for them. It saved us time as well. We didn't have to go through a long-winded presentation about how the business worked. We could make our judgments based on more pertinent information.

Today's challenge

As you look over or add to your prospect list, pay particular attention to those individuals who have had previous experience with network marketing. Make a special effort to recruit them through follow-up calls. You can also use this information as a point of connection. For example, you can say, "Hey, I know you understand how great the industry is" or "You and I have something in common." These are the people to target within your list as you cultivate your handful of winners.

Suggested readings: Although we don't know of any one book that deals exclusively with recruitment of veteran network marketers, you can glean the information you need from the books we've noted in previous Challenges. That's why we suggest you return to our book, as well as the books by Zig Ziglar, Mark Yarnell, Richard Poe and others. Kim Klaver has another book worth perusing: *Do You Have a Plan B? A guide to an alternative career in direct sales and network marketing.*

Challenge #19
Pick from the family tree

Now that you've looked over your present list, you likely will be asking, as we did, "How do I find more of these individuals?" Wouldn't it be great if there were just a whole long list of them? Good news! There is one. In fact, there are hundreds of them, and they're called genealogy reports.

To better understand how a genealogy report works, think first of your family tree. At the top, you have your grandparents, perhaps your great-grandparents. Beneath them, you have their descendants, which will include your parents, siblings and assorted aunts, uncles, cousins, etc. These relationships constitute your genealogy. Now imagine you are tracing descendants within a network marketing company. Its founders are like the grandparents; its first line of distributors are like the parents; the second, third, fourth levels and so forth, are like the siblings and cousins. Each of these descendants is listed in a company's genealogy report. Depending on the list, their number may range from the hundreds to thousands — *all* of them experienced network marketers.

Genealogy lists become available when a company closes its doors, goes belly-up, etc. You can purchase them from list brokers. Lists prices range, depending on the broker, but they are usually inexpensive for the number of leads provided. (The per-name costs often amounts to mere cents.) To find such brokers, do an Internet search. Type in "genealogy reports," "network marketing," "mlm" or some other such combination, and you'll be linked to hundreds of sources.

At this point, you might be wondering why you should buy a report that others are also buying? Doesn't that mean there will be no prospects left by the time you make contact? Again, that's a question we can't fully answer, but we do know this: No matter how many network marketers buy such a list, only a fraction of them will actually contact the leads on it. We find this astounding, but it certainly helps explain why so few network marketers succeed in this business: They're the only ones making the calls!

Here's another reason to not worry about your competition. You all have an equal shot. Just because someone else gets to a lead first doesn't mean they have an edge. Prospects turn down business opportunities all the time. Perhaps they've already signed with a company, have taken a hiatus or have personal issues that preclude them from even considering an offer. Their circumstances may well have changed by the time you make *your* first call (or subsequent ones). Meanwhile, your competitor may have taken no action or let too much time pass between follow-ups.

Ideally, you should purchase the most recent genealogy reports possible, but don't discount those that have been around awhile. Again, people change their minds, and sometimes it takes years before they do so.

Today's challenge

Go online and do a search for "genealogy reports marketing." (If you leave off "marketing," you will get sites on family genealogies.) Don't be overwhelmed by the number of hits your search finds. Concentrate on the first few pages. Visit the most promising pages to assess what they offer and how their prices and services differ.

How do you determine which lists are good? Unfortunately, there's no definitive way of knowing. Certainly, you should ask your sponsor or colleagues for recommendations. Ultimately, however, you'll need to give a broker a whirl. Again, genealogy reports are relatively inexpensive, and unlike opt-in and other types of mailing lists, the names on them are of *actual* network marketers.

Suggested readings: In our book *Absolutely* Everything *You Need to Know About Prospecting,* we discuss the pros and cons of using lists in general (Pages 142–145). On Pages 174–178, we also share our thoughts about Internet-based opt-in lists, aka prequalified or permission-marketing lists. There are pros and cons to these lists as well, which makes it all the more important to read this section. To learn even more about the subject, refer to *Permission Marketing: Turning strangers into friends and friends into customers* by Seth Godin.

Challenge #20
Network

Now it's time to discuss one of your most powerful marketing tools: networking. Too few network marketers make use of it. Perhaps they're shy ("Oh, I can't talk to strangers!") or lazy ("Hey, why's the word 'work' in network marketing?"). Perhaps they think it will require them to be someone they're not ("I'm not a born schmoozer") or that they'll have to do something they dislike ("I hate glad-handing"). We think they're wrong. Why else would the word "network" be in network marketing?

Please note that networking is not about making contacts so that you can use people to serve your purposes. Networking is about creating a mutually beneficial relationship in which each party helps the other. Results are not guaranteed. That's because the relationship is based on the "you," rather than on the "me." Help others achieve their goals, and they'll want to help you achieve yours. For example:

Say you work for a company that offers long-distance telephone services. At a Friends of the Library meeting, you begin talking with a woman who happens to be an optometrist. You make a mental note of this, not because you want to recruit her but because you might know some people who could use her services. Over the course of the next few months, you send several people her way. She's grateful for the referrals and makes mental notes as well. Perhaps she'll run across patients looking for long-distance service; she might be looking for it herself. Yours will be the name that pops into her mind.

Here, neither you nor she initiated the relationship as a means to generate business. You were merely two people who connected and then extended that connection to others. That is the beauty of networking. It's a natural, feel-good kind of prospecting: a win-win all the way around.

In addition to friends-of-the-library meetings, there are numerous "hot spots" in which to network one-on-one. For example, many Chambers of Commerce and professional groups and associations hold monthly get-togethers so individuals can meet, exchange business cards and leads, etc. You might also want to join or form a group whose sole purpose is to generate business for its members. These groups might have as few as six members, each of whom is from a different profession (sales, accounting, real estate, health care, etc.). Group members commit to swapping leads by passing one another's business cards to at least two other contacts per week.

To the greatest extent possible, network strategically with movers and shakers. This suggestion forms the basis of Dr. Thomas J. Stanley's book *Networking with the Affluent*.

Stanley, the co-author of the bestseller *The Millionaire Next Door: The surprising secrets of America's wealthy*, defines networking as a means of "influencing the people who influence the patronage behavior of dozens, hundreds, even thousands of affluent prospects." These are the very prospects we all aim to recruit. In fact, many of our industry's top earners devote their efforts exclusively to reaching this group.

According to Stanley, the best networkers succeed because they offer more than conventional products and services. They offer themselves by serving others in extraordinary and memorable ways.

Stanley's book is full of detailed illustrations of how this process works. For our purposes, however, we'll summarize what he identifies as the 12 rules of networking.

First, you identify individuals who belong to the "influence network" from which you want to recruit. Second, align yourself with those within the network who will help you gain entry to it. Third, do all you can to help others in the group succeed in ways they consider important. Fourth, be patient. Instead of expecting immediate payoffs, concentrate on long-term results. Payback, so to speak, takes time.

Fifth, spend more time with opinion leaders of the influence network than you would with your colleagues and peers. Sixth, "[s]olicit and obtain business for members of your influence network," rather than for yourself. In other words, become a facilitator by helping networkers connect with each other.

Seventh, raise your profile by sending network members clippings, notes and other materials that relate to their interests; sing their praises to other network members.

Eighth, interact, entertain and engage. Take advantage of social situations that draw network members together. For example, ask them to play golf, go to a concert or join you for dinner. Ninth, join other influential networks and serve as a bridge between them. Tenth, to maintain your credibility, recommend to network members only those individuals and/or companies that provide knockout service.

Eleventh, "donate your intelligence." For example, volunteer to lead seminars that spotlight your expertise or lend your skills to fund-raising drives for causes your influence network embraces. Twelfth, recruit new members to the network, allowing you even greater opportunities to make use of Rules 1–11.

We think Stanley's ideas and book are brilliant, but what if you don't have access to the affluent networks he writes about? Are you out of luck? Heavens, no! We certainly weren't members of such groups when we started out. We knew, however, that our position was to a great extent a reflection of our beliefs. If we believed we were below others, that's where we'd remain. That's why we began purging all self-limiting thoughts from our minds (as we discuss in

Challenge #21). That's also why we purposely prospected those above us economically. Each of these new customers and distributors raised us yet another level, expanding our influence network. In fact, about half of our best distributors had high-powered, lucrative careers before they joined our organization. Accordingly, they didn't have trouble envisioning financial success. Better still, they were realistic about what it would take to build their business. In short, they were serious players. They expected to make thousands or millions of dollars.

Today's challenge

Review your prospect list. Identify those individuals who are successful business people. Choose three, and put them at the top of your list. After you contact them, identify another three, and so forth. If you do not have such people on your list, brainstorm ways to meet them. What groups should you join or functions should you attend so you can meet with this key group of recruits? Make arrangements today for at least one such social interaction.

Suggested readings: Obviously, you need to get hold of a copy of Dr. Thomas J. Stanley's book, *Networking with the Affluent.* Here are other books about networking, as well as tips on mingling with greater confidence and flair: *Making Your Contacts Count: Networking know how for cash, clients and career success* by Anne Baber and Lynne Waymon; *Power Networking: Secrets for personal and professional success* by Donna Fisher; *The Confident Schmoozer* by Beth Mende Conny; and *How to Work a Room: The ultimate guide to savvy socializing in person and online* by Susan RoAne.

Challenge #21
Think positive

You have now come to what we believe is the most important Challenge. It can be summed up in a single word: belief. After more than 35 years in the business, we credit all of our achievements to that one word.

Belief, however, is not something you can learn by rote or plan. It rises slowly from within, like the sun at dawn, brushing away the shadows and revealing a world full of possibilities.

Each day, when we rise, we find greater possibilities still. For this, we have to thank our many "teachers" — the take-charge, positive-thinking individuals whose wise words and courageous acts allowed us to see beyond our horizons. Through their tapes, books and our personal associations, we've come to understand that everything's possible if you believe it is. How simple a concept! How challenging, as well. To act on your belief is akin to working without a net. What if you fall? Ah, but what if you don't? What if, instead, you form wings and soar to the greatest of heights?

Even as children, we pondered how others had achieved great wealth. Were they born into it? Did they possess a special gene or God-given talent? Were they just lucky? With time, we learned the answers.

Yes, some individuals are born into wealth; a greater number, however, come from modest or less-than-modest means. Their wealth is self-made, born of vision and hard work.

No, there is no gene that sets the wealthy apart from the not-so-wealthy. Biologically, we are all alike. No one is born with a lock on talent. God gave each of us many talents, and it is our duty to use them.

The answer is yes, and no, regarding luck. Sometimes events conspire in positive ways. To a greater degree, however, we make our own luck. We create wealth through our mind-set. Think rich and you will draw riches to you.

While some of these riches can be measured in dollars and cents, others are measured by our quality of life. Doing what you love, being with those you love, having the time and space to enjoy the world around you — these are gifts that money can't buy. Nonetheless, with the right attitude, you can have them all — and then some. Believing makes it so. If at first you don't succeed, you're running about average. That's one of our favorite quotes, and we share it often with those new to network marketing. As we impress upon them, there's no such thing as overnight success, just a whole lot of daytime and nighttime victories.

To be victorious, you must accept the challenges ahead. There will be times when you will question yourself. It would be abnormal if you didn't. But don't succumb to the response of so many, which is to walk away. Failure is not due to a lack of success, but to a lack of effort. That's why it's so important that you hang in there one moment longer. That one moment can change your life.

Today's challenge

Believe! We know it's easier said than done, but there is so much that you can do to create a winning mind-set. Here are but a few suggestions.

Find people who support your dreams. Don't squander your energy on those who undermine your efforts. These naysayers offer nothing but endless reasons why you'll fail. Before you know it, you're running scared and fast losing sight of your goals.

Unfortunately, you can't purge all of these people from your life — there are far too many of them. Fortunately, you can minimize their influence by drawing positive thinkers into your life. These individuals are dreamers and doers. They want what you want, a rich, full life — and they're willing to go after it.

Some of these thinkers may well be in your immediate circle. Others may be down the block, one seat over on a bus or at your next prospecting meeting. Because you'll never know for sure, keep your eyes, ears and mind open. You'll recognize them in a flash. They have a way of walking, talking and smiling that sets them apart. You'll be kindred souls.

Add positive thinkers to your life by becoming an avid reader, listener and viewer. Bookstore and library shelves are filled with excellent titles on self-development, visualization, goal-setting and the like. Their authors make great company and offer invaluable words of wisdom. Spend a bit of time with them each day, and you'll find yourself on the fast track to success.

Also make it a habit to listen to motivational audiocassettes and CDs. Doing so will turn even the most mundane tasks (e.g., commuting, dishwashing, etc.) into fun activities. And don't forget videocassettes and DVDs. Why watch ordinary TV when you can watch programming that inspires you to live an extraordinary life?

Adopt the gratitude attitude. We first learned of this law when reading *The Science of Getting Rich* by Wallace D. Wattles. According to Wattles' law, strong and constant gratitude attracts what you want out of life. It is what connects you to the universal spirit. "It is like sending a thank-you note to a friend for their thoughtful gift, for which they, in turn, will acknowledge you with a return letter or a telephone call." In other words, the universe responds with gifts of its own.

Gratitude is important because it gives birth to faith. "The grateful mind continually expects good things, and expectations becomes faith," Wattles wrote. "One who has no feeling of gratitude cannot long retain a living faith — and without faith you cannot get rich by the creative method." Why cut yourself off from the world's riches?

That's why we suggest you add a section in your notebook in which you list all of the good things in your life. Make your entries each night so you will awake with a positive mind-set. Do this for several days and you will understand just how many things you have to be grateful for.

Keep your word. People of integrity keep their word to others; they also keep their word to themselves. Put another way, they follow through on their dreams.

Dreams are promises; they are meant to be realized, not broken. They are meant to be acted upon. Act, and you will become a magnet, attracting the very things you've dreamed of. Once you touch them, your dreams become more fully charged, and the things you want come to you more and more quickly.

Suggested readings: Where do we even begin to list the many books on this topic that we have read over the years and which should become part of your library? Any such list would be incomplete, for when it comes to personal empowerment books, we discover (and devour!) new ones daily. We are going to limit ourselves to only five, all of which are self-improvement classics:

1. *The Science of Getting Rich,* by Wallace D. Wattles (a unique and compelling approach to achieving wealth).
2. *As a Man Thinketh,* by James Allen (standard reading for everyone who is serious about living the life of their dreams).
3. *The Power of Positive Thinking,* by Norman Vincent Peale (considered by some to be the greatest inspirational bestseller of all time).
4. *Think and Grow Rich,* by Napoleon Hill (another classic that has launched the careers of millionaires around the world).
5. *Psycho-Cybernetics,* by Maxwell Maltz (an invaluable exploration of the science of success).

Bibliographies and Web sites*

Bibliography of books mentioned in *The 21-Day Challenge*

— Allen, James. *As a Man Thinketh.* (G.P. Putnam's Sons)

— Aslett, Don. *Clutter's Last Stand: It's time to de-junk your life!* (Writers Digest Books)

— Baber, Anne, and Lynne Waymon. *Making Your Contacts Count: Networking know how for cash, clients and career success.* (Amacom)

— Conny, Beth Mende. *Believe in Yourself.* (Peter Pauper Press)

— Conny, Beth Mende. *The Confident Schmoozer.* (Blue Island Productions)

— Conny, Beth Mende. *Dare to Believe.* (Peter Pauper Press)

— Covey, Stephen. R., with A. Robert Merrill and Rebecca R. Merrill. *First Things First.* (Fireside)

— Fisher, Donna. *Power Networking: Secrets for personal and professional success.* (Bard Press)

— Gage, Randy. *How to Build a Multi-level Marketing Machine.* (Prime Concepts Group)

---

* The lists of books and Web sites we provide are only a few of the thousands of resources available to you. Should any of the books not be readily available, they can be special-ordered or purchased through Amazon.com and other online bookstores. Many of the titles will be discounted; used copies may also be available, some at greatly reduced prices. Should a book be out-of-print, you can go to sites that specialize in used books, such as powells.com or alibris.com. Finally, some of the books we list are self-published. Should you have trouble finding them, conduct a Web search using the author's name and/or the title of the book.

— Gawain, Shakti. *Creative Visualization: Use the power of your imagination to create what you want in your life.* (New World Library)

— Godin, Seth. *Permission Marketing: Turning strangers into friends and friends into customers.* (Simon & Schuster)

— Hernacki, Mike. *The Ultimate Secret to Getting Absolutely Everything You Want.* (Berkley Publishing Group)

— Hill, Napoleon. *Think and Grow Rich.* (Ballantine Books)

— Jeffers, Susan, Ph.D. *Feel the Fear ... and Beyond: Mastering the techniques of doing it anyway.* (Random House)

— Jeffers, Susan, Ph.D. *Feel the Fear and Do It Anyway.* (Ballantine Books)

— Johnson, Russ, and Usa Johnson with Beth Mende Conny. *Absolutely Everything You Need to Know About Prospecting.* (Advanced Business Corporation and Biz Builders Consulting)

— King, Charles, Ph.D. *The New Professionals: The rise of network marketing as the next major profession.* (Prima)

— Kiyosaki, Robert T. *Rich Dad, Poor Dad: What the rich teach their kids that the poor and middle class do not!* (Warner Books)

— Kiyosaki, Robert T. *The Business School for People Who Like Helping People: The eight hidden values of a network marketing business, other than making money.* (Cashflow)

— Klaver, Kim. *Do You Have a Plan B? A guide to an alternative career in direct sales and network marketing.* (Max Out Productions)

— Klaver, Kim. *The Truth: What it really takes to make it in network marketing.* (Max Out Productions)

— Laggos, Keith B., Ph.D. *Direct Sales: An overview.* (EEE, Inc.)

— Lesonsky, Rieva. *303 Marketing Tips Guaranteed to Boost Your Business.* (Entrepreneur Media, Inc.)

— Maltz, Maxwell. *Psycho-Cybernetics.* (Pocket Books)

—Parker, Roger C. *Relationship Marketing on the Internet.* (Adams Media)

— Levinson, Jay Conrad and Charles Rubin. *Guerrilla Marketing Online Weapons.* (Houghton Mifflin Company)

— Peale, Dr. Norman Vincent. *The Power of Positive Thinking.* (Ballantine)

— Poe, Richard. *Wave 3: The new era in network marketing.* (Prima.)

— Poe, Richard. *Wave 4: Network marketing in the 21st Century.* (Prima.).

— McGee-Cooper, Ann. *Time Management for Unmanageable People.* (Bantam.).

— Ries, Al and Laura Ries. *The 11 Immutable Laws of Internet Branding.* (Harper Business)

— RoAne, Susan. *How to Work a Room: The ultimate guide to savvy socializing in person and online.* (HarperResource)

— Robbins, Anthony. *Awaken the Giant Within: How to take immediate control of your mental, emotional, physical and financial destiny.* (Free Press)

— Roth, Eileen. *Organizing for Dummies.* (Hungry Minds, Inc.)

— Schiffman, Stephen. *Cold Calling Techniques (That Really Work!).* (Adams Media Corporation)

— Schiffman, Stephen. *Power Sales Presentations: Complete sales dialogues for each critical step of the sales cycle.* (Adams Media Corporation)

— Stanley, Dr. Thomas J., and William D. Danko. *The Millionaire Next Door: The surprising secrets of America's wealthy.* (Pocket Books)

— Stanley, Dr. Thomas J. *Networking with the Affluent.* (McGraw-Hill Trader)

— Stern, Isaac, with Chaim Potak. *Isaac Stern: My first 79 years.* (Alfred A. Knopf)

— Tracy, Brian. *Goals: How to get everything you want — faster than you thought possible.* (Berret-Koehler)

— Traverso, Debra Koontz. *How to Write a Compelling 30-second Commercial of Yourself.* (Blue Island Productions)

— Wattles, Wallace D., and Dr. Judith Powell. *The Science of Getting Rich.* (Top of the Mountain Publishing)

— Whiteley, Richard C. *The Customer Driven Company: Moving from talk to to action.* (Perseus Publishing)

— Yarnell, Mark. *Your Best Year in Network Marketing: How to achieve the financial success you deserve.* (Paper Chase Press)

— Yarnell, Mark, and Rene Reid Yarnell. *Your First Year in Network Marketing.* (Prima)

— Ziglar, Zig. *Goals: Setting and achieving them on schedule.* (audio, Nightingale-Conant)

— Ziglar, Zig. *Network Marketing for Dummies.* (Hungry Minds, Inc.)

Bibliography of network marketing books

— Adams, Garrett. *MLM (Multi-level Marketing) Made E-Z.* (Made E-Z Products)

— Barrett, Tom. *Dare to Dream and Work to Win: Understanding the dollars and sense of success in network marketing.* (Blue Ribbon Video)

— Butwin, Robert. *Street Smart Network Marketing: A no-nonsense guide for creating the most richly rewarding lifestyle you can possibly imagine.* (Prima)

— Fogg, John Milton. *Conversations with the Greatest Networker in the World.* (Prima Lifestyles)

— Gage, Randy. *How to Build a Multi-level Marketing Machine.* (Prime Concepts Group)

— Johnson, Russ, and Usa Johnson with Beth Mende Conny. *Absolutely Everything You Need to Know About Prospecting.* (Advanced Business Corporation and Biz Builders Consulting)

— Johnson, Usa Johnson with Beth Mende Conny. *Success is Yours with Network Marketing: 10 key steps to build your business.* (Advanced Business Corporation)

— King, Charles, Ph.D. *The New Professionals: The rise of network marketing as the next major profession.* (Prima)

— Kiyosaki, Robert T. *The Business School for People Who Like Helping People: The eight hidden values of a network marketing business, other than making money.* (Cashflow)

— Klaver, Kim. *Do You Have a Plan B? A guide to an alternative career in direct sales and network marketing.* (Max Out Productions)

— Klaver, Kim. *Rules for the New New MLMer.* (Max Out Productions)

— Klaver, Kim. *The Truth: What it really takes to make it in network marketing.* (Max Out Productions)

— Laggos, Keith B., Ph.D. *Direct Sales: An overview.* (EEE, Inc.)

— Maloney, Dale. *I Could Have Quit $10,000,000 Ago.* (Unknown)

— Morrison, James L. and Stewart Taub. *The Mission, The Method, The Magic: The insight on network marketing.* (Millennium)

— Paley, Russ. *Network Your Way to Millions: The definitive step by step guide to wealth in network marketing.* (Wealth Building Publications)

— Poe, Richard. *Wave 3: The new era in network marketing.* (Prima)

— Poe, Richard. *Wave 4: Network marketing in the 21st Century.* (Prima.)

— Pritchard, Paula. *Owing Yourself.* (Encore Management Group, Inc.)

— Rubino, Joe. *Secrets of Building a Network Marketing Organization from a Guy Who's Been There Done That and Shows You How to Do It Too.* (Upline Press)

— Rubino, Joe. *Ten Weeks to Network Marketing Succes: The secrets to launching your very own million-dollar organization in a 10-week business-building and personal-development self-study course.* (Vision Works)

— Schreiter, Tom. *Big Al's How to Create a Recruiting Explosion.* (Kaas)

— Schreiter, Tom. *Big Al's Super Prospecting: Special offer and quick-start programs.* (Kaas)

— Schreiter, Tom. *Big Al's Tells All: The recruiting system.* (Unknown)

— Scott, Gini Graham. *Get Rich Through Multi-level Selling: Build your own sales and distribution organization.* (Self Counsel)

— Scott, Gini Graham. *Strike it Rich in Personal Selling: Techniques for success in direct sales, multi-level and network marketing.* (Avon)

— Ward, Randy. *Winning the Greatest Game of All: The new era in multi-level marketing.* (Network Support Group)

— Yarnell, Mark. *Your Best Year in Network Marketing: How to achieve the financial success you deserve.* (Paper Chase Press)

— Yarnell, Mark, and Rene Reid Yarnell. *Your First Year in Network Marketing.* (Prima)

— Yarnell, Rene Reid. *The New Entrepreneurs: Making a Living—Making a Life Through Network Marketing.* (Quantum Leap)

— Ziglar, Zig. *Network Marketing for Dummies.* (Hungry Minds.)

Web sites*

If we were to list every Web site that would help you grow yourself and your business, we'd be at it for years. There are literally millions of sites out there, with hundreds of thousands being launched annually. For example, go into a search engine and type in "network marketing," and you'll come up with 8.7 million. Do the same search tomorrow, and you'll find that the number has increased. How then do you find the information you need? We offer these suggestions.

Set aside time. Unless you already know the site you will visit, prepare to spend time sorting through individual sites. There's simply no way around this. However, you can greatly reduce your time by conducting a more specific search. For example, instead of searching under "network marketing," search under "network marketing health products." Warning, you'll still get a lot of hits — 4.4 million to be exact. Accordingly, be even more specific. For example, when we typed in the name of Usa's company and one of its products, we got only 5,370 hits. That number is more manageable, especially if you restrict yourself to, say, the first 10, 30 or 50 hits listed. (Another warning: Just because a site is listed first, second or 10th doesn't mean it's the best in its class. It could mean the party paid for placement.)

---

* *Please note: We are not endorsing any of the sites we have listed; we are merely suggesting that they contain information you may find useful. We also list them as examples of the numerous types of sites — training, books, leads, etc. — available to you.*

Search by name. If there is a specific company you're interested in, type in its name and quickly skim the listings for the corporate site. Usually, it will be listed simply, such as "XXXX.com." If you'd like to learn more about a particular distributor, search by the names of both the company and individual.

Get recommendations. Ask your distributor and colleagues for their site recommendations. For example, we often mention the following sites:

- *www.amazon.com* — "library" research tool
- *www.alibris.com* — an online used book store
- *www.artofschmooze.com* — conversational skills primer
- *www.entrepreneur.com* — articles for new/small businesses
- *www.firstairmarketing.com* — leads and genealogy reports
- *www.fortunenow.com* — motivational programs
- *www.mlm911.com* — how-to articles, books, training
- *www.nightingale.com* — motivational tapes, CDs, etc.
- *www.successlists.com* — links to Wayne Dyer, Zig Ziglar, etc.
- *www.writedirections.com/tweak.html* — Web writing made easy
- *www.yahoo.com* — search engine with business forums

And don't forget our site: *www.theprospectpro.com!*

Have fun. The World Wide Web is an incredible place to visit. Once you become an experienced surfer, you'll find it an invaluable tool. With just a few keystrokes, you gain access to information and people you might never have found, not just in this country but across the globe. What a magical and fun experience!

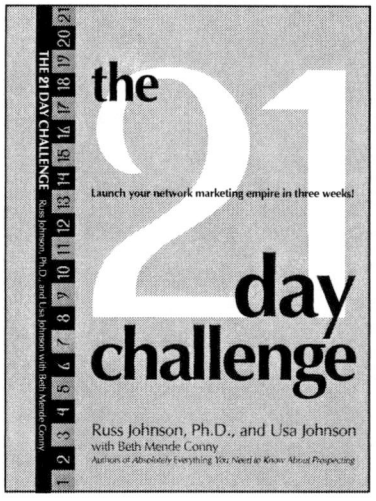

Five ways to use these books to build your business!

#1 — Give prospects a promotional gift that retains its effectiveness months — even years — from now.

#2 — Present your business opportunity in a professional, nonpressured way.

#3 — Educate others about how network marketing *really* works.

#4 — Train your downline by making the books required reading.

#5 — Inspire and motivate distributors, customers *and* yourself!

Want to read sample chapters? ... Place your order? ... Get information on bulk orders?

Visit **www.TheProspectPro.com**

Or contact Beth Mende Conny at:
Biz Builders Consulting, LLC
P.O. Box 1936
Frederick, MD 21702
301/694-9921
Beth@BizBuildersConsulting.com